EVERYMAN'S
BIBLE
COMMENTARY

JOEL, OBADIAH AND MICAH

To Scott & Jane,

May the Lord bless your ministry together in directing others to the Savior.

Vernon J. Finley

EVERYMAN'S BIBLE COMMENTARY

JOEL, OBADIAH AND MICAH

Thomas J. Finley

MOODY PRESS
CHICAGO

ISBN: 0-8024-2097-4

1 3 5 7 9 10 8 6 4 2

Printed in the United States of America

In memory of Dr. Charles Lee Feinberg,
beloved teacher and colleague

CONTENTS

PREFACE

People have been writing commentaries on parts of the Bible since before Scripture was completed. The earliest known commentaries include interpretations of parts of the prophetic books by the community that produced the Dead Sea Scrolls before Christ was born. That is a rather humbling thought as I offer this small token to the vast literature that has been produced since the first century B.C.

A commentary such as this should assist the reader to understand the biblical text in five ways. First, this commentary should clarify what is difficult to understand, especially for the reader who has no special training in the biblical languages or in theology. Second, a good commentary should serve as a guide to the variety of interpretations that may exist for any given passage. I have usually expressed my own views, but I hope that I have given enough information about the pros and cons that readers can enter into the process for themselves. Third, the commentary should give important background information so that the reader can interpret the text in light of its original setting. Fourth, some guidance should be given as to how the passage fits in with the rest of the Bible, both Old and New Testaments. Fifth, a useful interpretation of the Bible suggests ways that the message has abiding significance for its current readers. If I have succeeded in meeting these goals, I will be satisfied that the effort was worthwhile.

Too many have helped me with this task to mention everyone, but I will single out a few who have been the most directly involved. First, I would like to thank Biola University and Talbot School of Theology for giving me the sabbatical that enabled me to devote time to the project. Three who have helped the most with critiquing the manuscript are Joy Mosbarger, a student; Jack Elwood, my pastor; and my wife, Anita. All three gave excellent suggestions and have undoubtedly made this commentary a better work.

My love for the Old Testament and the Hebrew language began when I was a student under Dr. Charles Lee Feinberg. His life was characterized by his unwavering belief that Scripture is the inspired, inerrant word of God, and he encouraged me through his example to strive for excellence in interpreting it. He believed that it is vitally important to hear exactly what the text has to say, both in its original context and in its application to everyday life. His home-going occurred when this book was in process, and it is to his memory that I dedicate it.

Joel

1

INTRODUCTION TO JOEL

Words both ancient and powerful grip the reader who will take the time to become acquainted with the prophetic books of the Old Testament. The prophets behind the books come from a variety of backgrounds. Some spoke in kings' palaces in eloquent tones; others were quite ordinary in speech and manner. Sometimes they saw elaborate visions and heard voices speaking; other times they report their messages more simply, yet always noting that they were from God.

If the success of a person is measured by the impact he has on later generations, then all the prophets were highly successful. In their own generations, however, they usually preached to plugged ears and hearts of stone. Their words were framed to have universal appeal; and, although they originally spoke to Israel and Judah, they still speak as God's mouthpieces to all people everywhere.

Joel is noteworthy because his audience apparently responded to his preaching by a public demonstration of repentance (see comments on 2:12–19). The Lord was gracious to His people because of it, but as with many revivals the spiritual effects were short-lived and penetrated to only a portion of the population. Regardless of where the interpreter places Joel in history, it is clear that the people of the generation that followed him needed to repent of their own rebellion against the Lord.

The Prophet and His Times

Joel remains a shadowy figure among the prophets. His name, a common one in Israel, means "the Lord is God."[1] Possibly Joel was a priest, for he had a strong interest in ritual fasting and prayer. Joel spoke of the elders and priests as important leaders in the community.

The book of Joel is perhaps the most difficult to locate in history. Since Joel does not state when he wrote it, interpreters are forced to rely on internal allusions. Joel deals with a locust plague, but such plagues were commonplace. Three of the most important opinions about the date of composition vary widely from each other:

835–796 B.C.	During the time when Joash (835–796 B.C.) was too young to govern the country, and the high priest Jehoiada did so in his place (2 Kings 11; 2 Chron. 23–24).[2]
About 775–725 B.C.	Roughly contemporary with Hosea and Amos.[3]
About 500 B.C.	Approximately contemporary with Zechariah.[4]

In the first chapter, priests and elders are prominent as leaders in Jerusalem (1:2, 9, 13, 14), and no king is mentioned anywhere in the book. The final chapter mentions, either historically or prophetically, a time when the inhabitants of Judah and Jerusalem were "scattered . . . among the nations" and sold into slavery, while the land was "divided up" (3:2). Joel accuses Tyre, Sidon, and Philistia of taking booty of gold and silver to their own palaces and selling the Judeans to the Greeks (vv. 4–6). Consequently, the descendants of these enemies will be returned to the Judeans, who will "sell them to the Sabeans, a nation far away" (v. 8). Finally, the Egyptians and Edomites will be judged in a special way, "because of violence done to the people of Judah, in whose land they shed innocent blood" (v. 19).

Since Judah and Jerusalem occupy the center of attention, the events of Joel clearly took place there after the division of the kingdom. If one focuses on the importance of the priests and elders and the lack of reference to a king, two periods become most likely: the era of the minority of Joash (835–796 B.C.), under the regency of the high priest Jehoiada (2 Kings 11); and the postexilic period, after 515 B.C., when the temple was rebuilt.[5]

This argument is based on the text not mentioning a king. It could be that Joel had no special reason to refer to the king. The elders had an important political role throughout the history of Israel (cf. 1 Kings 20:7–8; 21:8, 11; 2 Kings 6:32; 10:1, 5; 23:1; 2 Chron. 34:29; Ezra 10:8, 14; Isa. 3:14; 9:15; 24:23; Jer. 19:1; 26:17; Ezek. 7:26).

More solid ground comes from considering the foreign nations Joel places together in chapter 3. The postexilic prophets Jeremiah (Jer. 47:4) and Zechariah (Zech. 9:2–6) single out Tyre, Sidon, and Philistia, and the Greeks are also mentioned in Zechariah 9:13. In fact, all the nations included in Joel 3 are also included in Zechariah 9–10, except for Edom. But Malachi, another postexilic prophet, does mention that nation. Thus, the data do not rule out the possibility of a postexilic date.

If Joel is postexilic, it might appear unusual that he does not mention Assyria, Babylon, or Persia. The postexilic prophet Zechariah, for example, mentions Darius the King of Persia (1:1) and Babylon (2:7). But perhaps Joel did not mention Babylon and Assyria because those nations had already fallen by the time of the Persian empire. The absence of Persia could simply reflect the generally positive relations with that nation, especially in the period of Zechariah (late sixth to early fifth centuries B.C.).

The similar configuration of nations seen in Joel 3 and in Zechariah 9–10 could easily support a date of about 500 B.C. for Joel. When Joel prophesies that Edom will become a "desert waste" (3:19) in the future, this may indicate a date prior to 500 B.C., for the kingdom of Edom was destroyed about that time.

Some appeal to allegedly late features in Joel's language to give the book an exilic or postexilic date. These features are not convincing enough to establish that Joel's language is in fact late.[6] Joel does use "Israel" to refer to God's people in general, rather than to the northern kingdom more specifically (2:27; 3:2; 3:16), but not in a manner that differs from the usage of certain preexilic prophets (cf. Isa. 1:3; Jer. 2:14; Amos 9:14–15; Mic. 1:13–15). The fact that so much of Joel is poetic could point to the preexilic period, though poetry is not absent from the postexilic prophets (cf. Zechariah 9–10). Various theological arguments that are sometimes raised as evidence of lateness are also not decisive.[7] But neither can one prove an early date from the thoughts and ideas of the book.

Some think that Joel's position among the twelve Minor Prophets indicates an early date for the book. The second half of the collection consists of late preexilic prophets (Nahum, Habakkuk, Zephaniah), followed by postexilic works (Haggai, Zechariah, Malachi), whereas the first half consists of the early preexilic books of Hosea, Amos, Jonah, and Micah. Shouldn't one expect Joel, positioned between Hosea and Amos, to be early also?[8]

In the Hebrew Bible, the entire collection of Minor Prophets was counted as one book, called "The Twelve," as early as about 190 B.C.[9] However, the sequence of the individual books does not appear to have stabilized until later. The Greek translation of the Old Testament has the order Hosea, Amos, Micah, Joel, Obadiah, Jonah for the first six, with the same order as the Hebrew Bible (and English versions) for the remaining books (Nahum, Habakkuk, Zephaniah, Haggai, Zechariah, Malachi). The variant orders indicates that it took some time for the precise order to become fixed.

Aside from Joel and Obadiah, whose dates are in dispute, an order from earliest to latest would be: Jonah, Amos, Hosea, Micah, Nahum, Zephaniah, Habakkuk, Haggai, Zechariah, Malachi. Moreover, Obadiah was most likely written in the early exilic period (see Introduction to Obadiah). Thus, at least some factors other than chronology must have been important for placing the twelve Minor Prophets in their present order.

The books without explicit details in their heading (first verse in the book) by which they can be dated were possibly put in order according to their topics. Jonah and Nahum both deal with Nineveh; Habakkuk and Zephaniah with Babylon. Also, Joel and Obadiah, in common with Amos, predict judgment on Edom.[10] (Incidentally, the doctrines of inspiration and canonicity deal with the original authors and the books to be included in the Bible, not their sequence. The order of books familiar to the English-speaking church is the product of some development over time.[11])

One final argument that figures largely in both preexilic and postexilic theories with respect to the date of Joel concerns literary relationships with other prophets. It soon becomes obvious to anyone who takes the time to make comparisons that many of the phrases and ideas in the book of Joel appear elsewhere. The problem is that it is extremely difficult to determine who quotes whom. The other prophets could have quoted Joel, or Joel could have quoted them.

Prophets who are completely original in their expressions are difficult to find. The Holy Spirit led the various prophets to develop different facets of similar truths in traditional language that appealed to the people. For example, many of the prophets describe the Day of the Lord in similar terms (cf. Isa. 13:6; Ezek. 30:2–3; Joel 1:15; 2:1–2; Amos 5:20; Obad. 15; Zeph. 1:15; Mal. 4:1, 5). This process extends even into the New Testament, where the book of Revelation makes numerous allusions to various Old Testament books, often using the same language (compare Rev. 9:20 with Deut. 4:28; Ps. 135:15–17; Jer. 1:16; Dan. 5:4; Mic. 5:13).

Whether Joel borrowed from other prophets or not, his book stands out as an original statement of the doctrine of the Day of the Lord. Moreover, Joel's language, if late, does not simply mimic what the other prophets say. Careful study shows many turns of phrase that are unique and fresh.

We know that Joel prophesied sometime between the division of the kingdom (about 930 B.C.) and the end of the canonical period (ca. 400 B.C.). If we must choose a more definite period, the best evidence points to a time close to 500 B.C. But John

Calvin wisely said, "As there is no certainty, it is better to leave the time in which [Joel] taught undecided; and, as we shall see, this is of no great importance."[12] In other words, the book deals with general material that can be interpreted successfully even if certainty about the date cannot be gained.

THE LITERARY CHARACTERISTICS OF JOEL'S BOOK

Joel, like most of the Old Testament prophets, wrote down most of his preaching in the form of poetry. Only the heading and 3:4–8 are in prose. Since the messages seem like sermons, he probably preached them before he transcribed them, though he might have adjusted the material some in writing the book.

By means of his well-constructed poems, Joel calls his audience to consider a recent disastrous locust plague, then pleads with them to repent, and finally warns them of dark days ahead. He delivers glad tidings of the Lord's renewed desire to bless them and proclaims a prophecy concerning the last days. His dramatic images draw the reader into personal participation. Joel moves his readers from horror and hopelessness to mourning and repentance, dread and awe, joy and assurance, hope and expectation. Through Joel, the Lord promises dreams and visions with the coming of the Spirit; and already in the book itself one sees visions of locusts that are like lions and an invading army, a temple that stands empty, a landscape stark as a dry desert, a darkness that overwhelms all light, a sky with perplexing signs, mountains with wine and milk pouring down their slopes, and a great judgment of nations in a large valley. Obviously one needs to approach the book with imagination and sensitivity regarding its poetic features.

A deeper question arises at this point concerning the relationship between the form of the book and its message. Already reference was made to the original oral setting of the presentations. Should we not expect, then, a strong homiletical style in which vivid word pictures prevail and a powerful current of emotions at times overwhelms the teaching? Joel pictures a world perched precariously on the brink of chaos, with nothing to hold it back but the grace of God alone. The reader will do well to reflect long on the utter suitability between forms of expression in Joel and the urgency of his message.

The Day of the Lord in Joel

Many of the prophets use the "day of the Lord" or similar expressions to refer to a future period of divine activity (cf. Isa. 13:6–11; Ezek. 30:2–4; Joel 2:28–32; 3:12–21; Amos 5:18–20; Obad. 15; Zeph. 1:14–15; Zech. 14:1–8; Mal. 4:5). In general the expression refers to the time at the end of history when God will bring judgment against the nations but salvation for His people. The events will continue through the establishment of the Lord's kingdom on earth until the final consummation of all things in the forming of new heavens and a new earth and the inauguration of the eternal state (cf. Zech. 14; 2 Peter 3:10).

A key part of the prophetic message concerns the need for people to evaluate whether or not they will experience judgment or salvation on the Day of the Lord. Amos's audience, for example, mistakenly looked forward to the Day of the Lord when they should have dreaded it because of their sins (Amos 5:18–20). Likewise, Joel presents both the prospect of judgment for Israel (1:15–2:11) as well as ultimate deliverance (chap. 3).

Joel centers his message around a single theme: the "day of the Lord." The first part of the book (1:1–2:27) deals with something that is already history, even to Joel: a great locust plague and a consequent drought that devastated the land of Judah. The effects were so severe that sacrifices could not be provided for the temple. Was this a sign that God had broken His covenant with Israel? Did it mean that Judah herself would be swallowed up in the Day of the Lord? Joel called on the people to repent, knowing that the Lord is gracious and compassionate (2:13). If the Lord would relent, the people could hope for fresh abundance from Him.

The last part of the book (2:28–3:21) turns to a time that is still future, even to us—that climactic era at the end of history when the Lord will judge the nations and restore Judah and Jerusalem to great prosperity. The locust plague typologically represented this future Day of the Lord. By intertwining the concepts of judgment and the Lord's response to repentance, Joel stresses that, although that day will be utter blackness, God will hear those who call on Him. Thus, the response of the Lord to Judah's repentance during the locust plague also *prefigures* His response to all Israel in the last days. God will destroy the nations who have harmed Judah just as He destroyed the locusts, and He will restore the fortunes of His people just as He made up for the devastation of the locusts.

The Message of Joel for Today

Joel's discussion of the "latter days" forms part of a larger series of revelations that give substance to what the believer can expect the Lord to do in the future. Even though the details apply specifically to the Jewish people, there is benefit for Christians as well. God makes His Spirit abundantly available in these last days, and He will be a refuge to all who call on Him (cf. Acts 2:14–39).[13] The practical value of prophecy is discovered when God's people live righteously in the face of opposition and struggle. Prophets like Joel show us the cosmic dimensions of life. We can cling to God's promises that there will be deliverance when the powers of this world are judged.

Several other themes in Joel have universal significance. The first half of the book especially brings out the way in which God is actively at work in all aspects of life. Even seemingly "natural" disasters are a part of His plan. Joel does not attempt to explore the precise reasons for the plague. It must be God's work because He controls everything. In the same way, renewed productivity of the land is a sign that God is blessing the people. Joel helps to underline God's control of the physical aspects of life in an age that increasingly seeks more scientific explanations. Such explanations are helpful, but Joel would point out that they do not really explain *why*, only *how*. Believers receive comfort as they contemplate, with Joel, how all things accomplish the purposes of the Lord (Rom. 8:28), working toward a conclusion in the return of Jesus Christ and the setting up of His kingdom.

Joel also teaches the importance of repentance and of regular communication with God. The greatest tragedy of the locust plague consists not in the loss of daily bread, but in the breaking of fellowship with God. In a similar way Jesus reiterated the words of Moses: "Man does not live on bread alone, but on every word that comes from the mouth of God" (Deut. 8:3; Matt. 4:4). Can there be any greater loss than for those in the church to find their prayers hindered by sin and lack of righteousness?

Finally, it is important to notice Joel's words of joy as well as of woe. Rampant suffering and sorrow in the land indicated to Joel that something was wrong. Gladness and joy ought to be the normal condition of God's people. The products of the land that come through cultivation and work are meant to be abundant and life sustaining. The Christian experiences a deep joy that goes beyond outward physical circumstances. Nevertheless, all that God provides in life is meant to eventuate in happiness and lasting satisfaction. The conclusions to both parts of Joel's book highlight the God who longs to show His lovingkindness and mercy through good gifts to His people.

STRUCTURE AND OUTLINE

The two parts of the prophecy correlate, demonstrating that Joel carefully laid out the plan of his book. The broad pattern is as follows:

Call to Repent (1:2–14)	**Gift of the Spirit (2:28–29)**
Day of the Lord (1:15–2:2a)	**Day of the Lord (2:30–32)**
The Lord's Army (2:2b–11)	**The Nations' Armies (3:1–3)**
The Lord's Covenant Mercy (2:12–14)	**The Lord's Covenant Concern (3:4–8)**
Call to Repent (2:15–17)	**Call to Holy War (3:9–11)**
The Lord's Response (2:18–20)	**The Lord's Response (3:12–17)**
Renewed Blessing (2:21–27)	**Renewed Blessing (3:18–21)**

The structure consists of a series of reversals. The locusts devastated the land, but the Spirit will usher in a new age of prophecy and blessing. The Day of the Lord in the first part of the book threatens to engulf Judah, but in the second part it overwhelms the nations. The mercy of the Lord occupies center stage in both parts of the book.

I. Locusts in the Land (1:1–14)
    A. Heading (1:1)
    B. Call to Attention (1:2–4)
    C. Call to Mourning (1:5–14)
II. Judgment in the Land (1:15–2:11)
    A. Aftermath of the Locust Invasion (1:15–20)
    B. Invasion of the Lord's Army (2:1–11)
III. Mercy in the Land (2:12–27)
    A. A Call to Repentance (2:12–17)
        1. Appeal to the Character of the Lord (2:12–14)
        2. Appeal for a Solemn Assembly (2:15–17)
    B. The Lord's Response (2:18–27)
IV. Wonders in the Earth (2:28–32)
    A. The Availability of God's Spirit (2:28–29)
    B. The Awesomeness of God's Presence (2:30–31)
    C. The Availability of God's Salvation (2:32)
V. Judgment in the Earth (3:1–21)
    A. The Lord Judges the Nations for Their Treatment of Israel (3:1–3)
    B The Lord Punishes Tyre, Sidon, and Philistia (3:4–8)
    C. The Lord Defeats the Nations but Delivers Israel (3:9–17)
    D. The Lord Blesses Judah but Makes Egypt and Edom Desolate (3:18–21)

2

LOCUSTS IN THE LAND

Joel 1:1–14

The overall structure of the book of Joel should be noted carefully. First, Joel describes how he pleaded for the people to mourn and fast. Then he informs his readers that God took pity on the people and removed the plague from their land (2:18–19).[14] A possible implication from the context is that Joel's preaching led to national repentance. Thus, the locust plague, the preaching of Joel, and the Lord's response in renewing the land comprise the full sequence of events that Joel calls the people to consider in his opening words.

Our prophet engenders a certain tension by plunging immediately into the preaching without setting any context. Yet 1:2–3 presupposes the entire story. How can the people hope to tell these things to future generations unless there will be a future? The locust plague brought the nation so close to destruction that it foreshadowed the imminent onset of the Day of the Lord. The command to make these events a part of the traditions meant that judgment has been stayed for now.

The first part of Joel's book (1:1–2:27) is organized around various commands and the descriptions that accompany them. The structure that results can be diagrammed as follows:

- Hear this! Listen! Tell! Locusts have devoured the crops. (1:2–4)
- Wake up! Wine has been cut off by the invaders. (1:5–7)
- Mourn! Offerings and libations have been cut off. (1:8–10)
- Despair! All plants and trees have perished. (1:11–12)
- Wail with sackcloth! Fast! Cry out to the Lord! Offerings and libations have been cut off; the Day of the Lord has come upon us. (1:13–20)
- Blow the trumpet! Sound the alarm! A large and mighty army has invaded. (2:1–11)
- Return to the Lord! Fast! Weep! Mourn! Rend your heart! He is gracious and compassionate. (2:12–14)
- Blow the trumpet! Fast! Call an assembly! Gather the people! Consecrate the assembly! Bring together the elders! Assemble everyone! The Lord might respond. (2:15–17)
- Do not be afraid! Be glad and rejoice! The Lord has done great things. (2:18–21)
- Do not be afraid! Pastures and trees have come back. (2:22)
- Be glad and rejoice! The Lord has given a sign of restoration. (2:23–27)

The second half of the book (2:28–3:21) is organized instead around phrases more typical of prophetic books:

- And afterward . . . (2:28)
- In those days and at that time . . . (3:1)
- In that day . . . (3:18)

In the first part Joel calls the people to repentance; in the second part he delivers messages about the future by quoting the Lord directly. Only in 3:9–13 do we find commands, but there they are issued by the Lord Himself.

Heading (1:1)

All of the twelve Minor Prophets, as well as the prophetic works of Isaiah, Jeremiah, and Ezekiel, have a heading that introduces the book. Joel's heading tells the reader only two things: this is God's word, and it was delivered through a certain Joel son of Pethuel. Since so many of the prophets give more details in a heading (but see Obadiah, Nahum, Habakkuk, and Malachi), why is Joel's so abbreviated? Perhaps Joel did not think it necessary for the reader to tie the message to a specific point in history.

The title of the book follows the general structure of several other prophetic books. Observe especially Hosea 1:1; Micah 1:1; and Zephaniah 1:1. The prophet spoke not on his own authority, but only at the impulse of the Spirit of the Lord. Since Joel's "word" applies to the whole book, here it means something like "message."

Call to Attention (1:2–4)

Joel calls for the leaders of the people to listen to his words and repeat them to their children, bringing to mind the instructions of Moses in Deuteronomy 6. According to this passage, the Israelites were perpetually to tell their children about the great commandment to love the Lord with all one's heart. Thus, the book of Joel is designed to teach a lesson. The locusts and drought threatened the existence of Judah, but if the people would repent, God could restore them. The Lord desired to imprint on the minds of all future generations how severe the catastrophe of the locust plague was and how He intervened to save the nation.

When Joel calls his listeners to "hear . . . [and] listen" (1:2), he follows a pattern familiar from prophetic and other forms of elevated speech (Gen. 4:23; Num. 23:18; Deut. 32:1; Judg. 5:3; Pss. 49:1; 84:8; Isa. 1:2, 10; 32:9; Hos. 5:1). It is striking how the "elders" are paired with "all who live in the land" (cf. 1:14). The construction implies, "Let all the leaders hear what I have to say. In fact, let the whole community listen."

After summoning the attention of his audience, Joel proceeds to summarize his message with a rhetorical question by which he strengthens the impression of complete devastation found in the following verses. The question can be resolved into something like, "This is the worst thing that has ever happened to us."

The events give such stunning evidence of the Lord's work in the nation that the people must pass them down from generation to generation. The Lord requires parents to pass along to their children historical memory of what He has done. For Christian parents this could include not only the events of Scripture, but also the history of the Lord's dealing with the parents or with their particular church tradition. Remembering the history of how the Lord has acted among His people is an activity widely practiced and commended in Scripture (see Deut. 1:6–4:38; Josh. 4:4–9; 24:3–13; Neh. 9:5–37; Ps. 74; Dan. 9:4–19).

Joel 1:4 contrasts with 2:14. The locusts leave nothing, but "who knows? [The Lord] may turn and have pity and leave behind a blessing." The stripping away of everything from the land shows that God's covenant blessing has been withdrawn. The pattern, "what X has left, Y has eaten," makes the reader think of a progression of different types or stages of locusts. Since 2:25 refers to "the years" that these various locusts ruined the fields, the catastrophe must have occurred over an extended period of time.

Many commentators agree that Joel describes a literal locust plague in the first chapter, though there is more dispute about the second chapter.[15] In chapter 2 Joel describes a situation that seems to go beyond what locusts might do, making some writers think it refers to a future invasion of the land by an army.[16] Joel may use some hyperbole (exaggerated language) when he describes the locust plague, as when he asks rhetorically whether anything like this has happened before. Hyperbolic language was common in Hebrew poetry and sometimes occurred in prose as well (see 2 Kings 18:5 and 23:25).[17] Locust plagues were greatly feared, and this particular one was unusually severe, as Joel stresses by his larger-than-life imagery.

Both chapters 1 and 2 describe a real infestation of locusts, though Joel sees that the plague foreshadows worse things to come. Today the people need to contend with locusts; tomorrow they may have to suffer the woes of the Day of the Lord.[18]

Call to Mourning, Fasting, and Public Assembly (1:5–14)

Joel calls the people to spend time in deep mourning, fasting, and public assembly. The devastation of the locusts demands drastic action, for the people could not survive on what the insects left behind. Even worse, they could not continue to offer sacrifices to the Lord. Hence, the plague threatened the very bond between God and people through the covenant.

When fasting is mentioned, it is clear that the mourning is for sin as well as for the tragedy that has struck the nation. In his final appeal Joel calls explicitly for repentance and prayer to the Lord (2:12–17). Between the two parts of his admonitions, however, he compares the magnitude of the disaster to the Day of the Lord (1:15–2:11). The only thing that might possibly avert such final judgment is a time of national lamentation and fasting, thus the urgency in his language.

The section divides into two parts: first, verses 5–12 call for grieving and mourning because of the tragedy; second, verses 13–14 introduce the burden of Joel's prophecy—the people of Judah must repent in response to what God has done. The first people Joel tells to mourn and weep are "drunkards" and "drinkers of wine" (1:5). Those addicted to wine must go to great lengths to obtain it (see Prov. 23:35), but not even they are able to find any. The abuser will be the most adversely affected, but even the occasional wine drinker will need to mourn his loss.[19]

At verse 6 Joel speaks of a "nation," anticipating the detailed description of the locust invasion in chapter 2. Eventually he will reveal that the insects foreshadow the time when the Lord will bring an invading army during the "great and dreadful day of the Lord" (2:31). Joel skillfully evokes both images.

Since God is the speaker in these verses (see 1:1), "my land" identifies Judah and Jerusalem as uniquely the Lord's (see "my holy hill," 2:1). The Lord frequently calls Israel "my land" in the prophets (see Jer. 2:7; 16:18; Ezek. 36:5; 38:16; Joel 3:2). The sequence "my land . . . my vines . . . my fig trees" (1:6–7) was surely intended to evoke the thought of Judah and the people who inhabited it. Fruitful vines and fig trees represented the blessing of the Lord on the land (1 Kings 4:25; Mic. 4:4; Zech. 3:10). When the vineyard is ruined, it means that God has taken the blessing from His people.

Joel envisions a tragic scene in verse 8: while the virgin waited expectantly for the day when her husband would take her to his home (Deut. 20:7), he suddenly died.[20] That is the depth of the sorrow Joel attempts to bring out. "Sackcloth" was made of goat or camel hair and worn during a time of mourning (see Gen. 37:34; 2 Sam. 3:31; Isa. 22:12; Amos 8:10). Goat hair would often be black, and either material could feel rough and uncomfortable if placed next to the body. Perhaps its simplicity also contributed to its symbolic association with mourning or with social protest.

Just as the priests at the temple (1:9) mourned because they could no longer be supported by the grain offerings and drink offerings (Lev. 2:3, 10), even so the betrothed virgin mourned for her husband who died even before the marriage could take place. She was now a widow lacking support, and the priests were in similar straits. Perhaps the "virgin" and the "husband" of verse 8 are meant to allude to the relationship between the Lord and Judah. If so, the plight of the priests in the Lord's house brings the figurative allusion into reality.

For the people as a whole, being without grain and drink offerings signified that God had rejected them. The worshiper probably expressed thanksgiving for a restored relationship with the Lord through the grain offering that would typically follow the burnt offering.[21] Libations of wine frequently accompanied various types of offering (see Lev. 23:13; Num. 15:5; 28:7). For the average Judean, accustomed on a regular basis to presenting a portion of the harvest, it must have been quite a shock to be unable to supply the Lord's portion, let alone have enough left to live on.

For stylistic and thematic reasons, 1:10–12 can be regarded as a unit within the larger section of 1:5–14. Verse 9 concludes with the introduction of the priests, and verse 13 returns to them. A high number of wordplays and patterns based on how the text sounds when it is read out loud (in the Hebrew) further serve to bind the unit together and give it aesthetic appeal.[22]

After Joel first introduces the problem of no agricultural products for sacrifices at verse 9, he then describes in detail the agricultural disaster (vv. 10–12) before pleading for prayer and fasting (vv. 13–14). The disaster encompasses the fields, the parched soil,[23] and all types of fruit. Consequently, the farmers and vine growers, having nothing to show for their work, must participate in ritual mourning, a rite that shows shame as well as sorrow (see Jer. 48:1–5). The joy of life for all people in the land becomes as dry as the dusty soil or the desiccated plants.

Verse 13 marks a turning point. First, the priests or ministers were said to be in mourning (v. 9); now they are commanded to lament to show their repentance and supplication. Joel addresses the religious leaders in order to draw the community into a demonstration of humble dependence on God. They should set the example and stir up the people. The situation is very severe; the attitude of mourning must continue through the night. It is not a time for normal activities in the temple, which are followed by a night of sleep. Twenty-four-hour vigilance is necessary to meet the emergency.

During this time the people must "cry out" to the Lord (v. 14). This term could be used of a national plea for deliverance (Ex. 2:23; Ps. 22:4–5). The narrator of Judges used it in describing the repentance of the people that preceded the appearance of a new judge (Judg. 3:9, 15; 6:6–7; 10:10). The term also occurs in the Psalms on a more personal level (Ps. 142:1, 5). The Lord would respond to such a cry only if the attitude of the heart was sincere (Hos. 7:14; 8:2–3; Mic. 3:4).

Joel's positive words about fasting (v. 14) balance some of the other prophetic condemnations of fasting. God is displeased when mere ritual is seen as a magical means of manipulating Him. Prophets such as Amos, Isaiah, and Zechariah rightly spoke against such misuse of established religion. Joel reminds the people, however, that rituals can be an appropriate method for demonstrating inward sorrow for sin and a desire to change. Fasting and the solemn assembly were proper ways for the community to show humility and submission to God in the face of national disaster, as long as they reflected the truth about the condition of the heart.

Previously Joel called on the elders and all the inhabitants of the land to pay attention to the Lord's word (1:2). When he calls upon them again (v. 14), it serves as a literary device known as *inclusio*. That is, when the beginning of a unit is echoed at its end by the same or similar wording, it sets off the entire section as a complete unit. This is also known as an "envelope structure." Verse 15 starts a new section of the book.

3

JUDGMENT IN THE LAND

Joel 1:15–2:11

Joel turns from his call for national repentance to describe in a new way the devastation of the locust plague and the drought that followed it. At the same time, he raises the fearsome possibility that the final destruction that accompanies the great and awesome Day of the Lord might be close behind (see discussion of 2:31).

Then, heightening the sense that Judah herself might be swallowed up in that day, Joel compares the locust infestation to an invasion by the Lord's army (2:1–11). If Joel wrote to a postexilic audience, his description would have stirred memories of the dreadful attack by the Babylonian army. Joel's listeners would be asking themselves, "Is the present disaster any less severe? Will the Lord destroy His people from the face of the earth?"

The chapter break occurs at 2:1 rather than at 1:15; yet when Joel mentions the Day of the Lord for the first time in 1:15, it surely indicates an important new thrust, especially since that day figures so prominently throughout the book. Thus, it appears better to break the thought at 1:15, with 2:1–11 an intensification of the motif of the Day of the Lord.

Aftermath of the Locust Invasion (1:15–20)

Joel surveys the devastation of his country and realizes how near total the destruction from the Lord is. The lack of food has harmed human and beast alike. Worst of all, the Lord must have withdrawn His presence for conditions to be so bad. No joyous sounds echo through God's house, and even the wild animals yearn for His presence.

Thus the tension rises: Does this ruin mean that the Day of the Lord has arrived? Will God cut Himself off completely from His people? The stress is nearly unbearable when Joel identifies the locusts with the Lord's army, but then the rest of the book shows a way out of the dilemma. First, when Joel returns to his call for repentance, he stresses the Lord's grace and mercy. Second, when Joel turns to the "great and dreadful day of the Lord" (2:31), it becomes clear that Israel, by the power of God's Spirit, will be delivered.

When the thought of the Day of the Lord first comes to Joel (1:15), the shock knocks all the wind out of him as he cries out "Alas!" The people know the terror of the locusts, but an even more frightening day is not far off. The awful fact cannot be described in any more desperate terms: the locust plague is the harbinger of the Day of the Lord. "We are in a state of total ruin now," says Joel. "What will happen when the Day of the Lord comes upon us?"

A play on words in the last line of verse 15 stresses the emotion of the situation: "destruction" (Heb., *shod*) will come from "the Almighty" (Heb., *Shaddai*). Perhaps "destruction from the Destroyer" would capture more of the flavor.[24] The language of the verse follows the wording of Isaiah 13:6 and Ezekiel 30:2–3 closely. The Day of the Lord was a traditional theme, and various prophets used a set of stock phrases to describe it. Ezekiel directs his prophecy against Egypt, whereas Isaiah speaks to Babylon. So Joel knew that the doctrine of the Day of the Lord was connected with a future time of judgment on the nations. He fears that the locust plague may be a sign that the Lord will treat Israel like any other nation.

In verses 16–18, Joel picks up the theme of verse 12, where he said that "rejoicing dries up from the sons of men" (NASB). When the people realize how the Lord has reacted to their sins, they lose the joy of their salvation. Later, Joel speaks of a renewal of joy when the Lord accepts Israel again (2:23).

As Joel builds to a climax, he cries out to God for deliverance (v. 19). None can help the struggling people and beasts in Judah except God alone. The plea for mercy here foreshadows the opportunity to find salvation during the calamitous time of the "great and dreadful day of the Lord" by calling on the Lord's name (2:32).

In the final two verses of the chapter, Joel closes out his general description of the damage by reiterating three areas of suffering: the pastureland with its low plants, the trees of the field, and the animals. The herdsmen in Judah concentrated their flocks in the wilderness area, which extended from the top of the Judean ridge eastward to the Dead Sea. The insects devoured the grass, and the pastures could not recover without rain.

The language of verse 20 closely resembles Psalm 42:1: "As the deer pants for streams of water, so my soul pants for you, O God." The comparison helps to highlight a unique feature of the Joel passage: the beasts pant for *God,* not for the water brooks. In this way the prophet stresses the dependence of all living things on their Creator. God has brought the calamity, and only He can remove it. The final phrase of the first chapter, "for fire has devoured the open pastures," closes out the petition that began with the same wording (v. 19), but it also makes an effective transition to the next chapter.

Fire occurs often in the Old Testament as a means of divine judgment (e.g., Gen. 19:24; Lev. 10:2; Num. 11:1; 16:35; Deut. 9:3; Pss. 11:6; 21:9; Jer. 4:4; Amos 1:4; Nah. 1:6; Zech. 11:1). The doubling of the statement about fire, then, highlights the judgment of the locusts and drought. The calamity came because of God's anger. In the same way Joel tells us in chapter 2 that the army of locusts is God's army (v. 11), with a consuming fire before and behind them (v. 3).

Invasion of the Lord's Army (2:1–11)

Joel, like other prophets of the Old Testament, connects the Day of the Lord with military action (3:9–12). Amos saw the day heavy with judgment for the northern kingdom of Israel (Amos 5:18–20), and he also predicted that a foreign army would invade the country (6:14). Zephaniah likewise foresaw invasions that would come with this day of judgment (Zeph. 1:16); and Ezekiel even applied the Day of the Lord to the Babylonian onslaught against Judah in 586 B.C. (Ezek. 13:5; see Dan. 11:41; Zech. 14:1–2).

Therefore, it is not surprising that Joel couches his description of the locust plague in terms of an army that the Lord Himself leads. Joel's point is not primarily to describe a future attack against Jerusalem. Rather, he intends to motivate the people to repent by showing how the invasion of locusts represents the Lord's judgment against the land. For the wicked, the Day of the Lord can only lead to complete destruction. If the Judeans remain in their sin, their end could be as final as that of the nations in the great period of God's wrath.

For Joel, then, the Day of the Lord is near ("is coming," "is close at hand," 2:1). That is, the locusts show that the Lord's anger against His people must be turned aside if the nation is to survive. That is why chapter 2 so vividly describes how the locusts enter the city. They bring divine judgment with them no less than the Assyrian or Babylonian armies, or than the enemy forces that will assemble against Israel at the end of the age. There is no defense against an army brought by the Lord, but Joel hopes to curb the full effects through a national repentance.

Certain key phrases link 2:1–11 with chapter 1: "the day of the Lord is near/coming" (1:15; 2:1); "a large and mighty army comes" (2:2; see 1:6); "such as never was of old" (2:2; see 1:2); and "before them fire devours" (2:3; see 1:19). Also, the Lord explicitly calls the locusts "my great army that I sent among you" (2:25), a clear echo of 2:11: "The Lord thunders at the head of his army." The verbs within 2:2–11 describe the locust invasion as though Joel is viewing it as it happens rather than as a past event. In this way Joel increases the vividness of the event, helping to stir the listeners to action.

This is not to deny the legitimacy of comparing the way in which the Lord brings the army of locusts and the armies that will invade Israel in the future. Joel's description of the locust invasion can be considered typological, with its correspondent in the latter days. The locusts are a harbinger of that day precisely because the Lord controls them in the same way that He will direct literal armies at that time. In fact, in the second half of the book Joel draws parallels between his own time and what will take place "afterward" (2:28). Even so, it is not necessary to think that Joel means *only* a real military incursion in 2:1–11.[25]

The first two verses of chapter 2 form an envelope structure *(inclusio)* with 2:11, enclosing the entire description within the topic of the Day of the Lord. Joel amasses a number of traditional phrases to describe the gloom and danger of that time.

First, he calls the people to prepare for an enemy invasion by blowing a trumpet or shofar, used as a signal to alert the population. Other prophets also associate the blowing of the trumpet and the cry of alarm with judgment from the Lord (Jer. 4:19; Hos. 5:8; Zeph. 1:16). The alarms do not call upon the people to prepare for an ordinary invasion. It is the Lord Himself who is near at hand with the full fury of His judgment.

The second verse symbolizes the judgment and wrath of the Day of the Lord by darkness (see Isa. 13:10; Amos 5:18, 20; Zeph. 1:15). For Amos (Amos 5:18), the darkness would engulf all the Israelites who smugly believed that the judgment would not touch them. Isaiah (Isa. 13:10) applied it to the Babylonians, though he also spoke of "a day of reckoning" (NASB) when the Lord will deal with Judah (2:12). Zephaniah (Zeph. 1:15) saw the darkness overwhelming the Judeans. For Joel, the approaching day potentially threatens Judah but need not overtake anyone who "calls on the name of the Lord" (2:32). Common to all these prophets is the idea that the Lord will judge sinners in an unprecedented manner.

The Day of the Lord, then, includes that time when God will come personally to deal with all sinners among the nations of the earth. It also encompasses a period of blessing that follows the judgment,[26] but Joel does not focus on this until chapter 3. Could this great darkness apply also to a literal locust plague?

Many have described the swarm as being like a dark cloud that obscures the light of the sun.[27]

With so much talk of darkness, the third line of verse 2 surprises the reader with the mention of "dawn." The point of the comparison is suddenness. Anyone who has seen a sunrise in the mountains knows how quickly the brightness appears on the face of the cliffs. That is how quickly the vast army of locusts appeared (see Isa. 58:8).

The army of locusts advances and burns everything in its path (2:3). Leslie Allen observes, "It is almost as if a fiery aura emanating from the advancing locusts sweeps ahead of them" (see Pss. 50:3; 97:3; Joel 1:19; Zeph. 1:18; Zech. 11:1; 12:6; Mal. 4:1).[28] The locusts destroyed all vegetation as surely as though an army had gone through and torched the fields. Perhaps the burning flame behind the army refers to the drought that made it impossible for the land to recover.

The exaggerated description of the land as "like the Garden of Eden" before the locusts came heightens the contrast with the barrenness afterward. Joel is quite interested in "before and after" descriptions, and they form a motif throughout the book. The locust plague is unequaled in past experience, and people will talk about it for generations to come. The Lord will restore the damage done by the locusts, turning the land once again into a paradise with plenty to eat (2:24–25). Of course, repentance represents a new condition for the people, and the Lord has also changed, speaking analogically, by turning from judgment to salvation.

The theme of reversal continues into the second half of the book with the actual appearance of the Day of the Lord. It will come about "afterward" (2:28) and will include spiritual blessings and salvation in great abundance. At that time also there will be awesome effects in nature and a great judgment, but God will deliver those of His people who call on Him. After the judgment Judah will become a land of unprecedented fruitfulness, whereas the nations who harmed her will become the "desolate wilderness" that she once had been (3:18–19, NASB). What had been "before" will be reversed in the time "afterward."

When the army is compared in appearance to horses, it

would seem that locusts are meant (2:4). It would be unusual to say that the people are like horses. Locusts resemble horses, and they move rapidly like war-horses.

The passage moves on from physical appearance (like "horses") to motion ("like cavalry") and then to sound (v. 5). Enemy chariots were heard many times jostling about on the Judean hills. The locusts made a similar sound as the swarms leaped from hilltop to hilltop (see Nah. 3:2). The terrifying sound of the locusts crescendos as the people in the city first hear the crackling of their fields falling to the insects and then the deafening roar of the swarm massed for the frontal assault. The terror shows in the facial expressions of everyone in the city (2:6).[29]

Not only do the locusts run like warriors, they climb walls like battle-hardened troops (2:7).[30] Locust swarms operate as a tight unit (see Prov. 30:27), even as a well-trained army marches in regular ranks (2:7–8). The locusts continue their march despite all efforts at resistance.

Verses 7b and 8a have an interesting chiastic (A–B//B′–A′) structure.

A   And-each in-his-ways they-march
        B   and-not they-deviate their-paths.
        B′   And-each his-fellow not they-jostle
A′   each in-his-road they-march

All four lines speak of regular ranks, but lines A and A′ stress predetermined paths, whereas B and B′ refer to the lack of moving outside those roads. This is a nice example of how the poetic form underlines the meaning. The insects march on in wave after wave in perfectly aligned ranks.

Houses were built close to or even right against the walls of cities in ancient times, so one should imagine the locusts scurrying around the walls to gain access to various parts of the city (2:9). The sequence of entering the city to breaching the wall to entering the houses has a climactic effect. The reader gradually feels the locusts getting closer and closer.

The effects of the shaking of the earth described in 2:10 may be local or universal (see 2:30–31). On a local level one should think of huge swarms, which send a quaking sensation through the land in their continual rhythm of alighting and rising. Also the beating of wings and rapid, sharp turns of the formation make the sky itself appear to shake. On the universal level the prophets apply similar language to the appearance of the Lord Himself, which causes an uproar in heaven and earth (see Jer. 4:23–28). It is not that the text has more than one meaning, but that the local plague stirs up thoughts of the greater events of the end. The coherence of the passage as a description of the locust plague suggests that the local significance is primary.

Even the reference to the darkening of the sun and the moon could refer to the immediate event. Eyewitness accounts of locust infestations mention a thick cloud that blocks out even the light of the sun.[31] Yet once again Joel's language prefigures images of the upheavals in the sky that accompany the final Day of the Lord (see Isa. 13:10; Zeph. 1:14–15).

The most important connection between the locusts that overran Judah in Joel's day and the future Day of the Lord is the personal presence of the Lord in both cases. That connection becomes prominent when Joel views the Lord as the Commander of the locust army (2:11). Joel pictures the shouting of the military commander to his troops in the heat of battle (see Jer. 4:16; Lam. 2:7). The Lord personally leads this army of locusts against Jerusalem and Judah; the element of judgment cannot be missed. Later Joel will turn the tables and depict the Lord roaring like a lion from the midst of Jerusalem in wrath against the nations (3:16). "His people," however, will find "refuge" in Him at that time.[32]

At the climax of his description, Joel refers once more to the terror of the Day of the Lord. It is great because it will include unusual events that will result in unbearable distress (see Jer. 30:4–7; Zeph. 1:14–18). It inspires such terror that the prophet cries out, "Who can endure it?" In like manner Amos saw Israel on the verge of destruction and exclaimed, "Sovereign Lord, I beg you, stop! How can Jacob survive?" (Amos 7:5). Joel means to say that if the locust plague blends into the great Day of the Lord, Judah cannot survive.

It is interesting to reflect on Joel's power as a preacher to motivate the people to repent on the basis of warning them of the judgment to come. Although the New Testament focuses on the Lord's grace and mercy, the warnings of judgment are not absent there either (cf. Matt. 24:42–51; 1 Thess. 5:1–11; Rev. 20:11–15). In light of Joel and the rest of Scripture, one might wonder whether contemporary pastors who tend to avoid "fire and brimstone" preaching in favor of a steady diet of mercy and forgiveness provide an incomplete presentation of God's Word.

4

MERCY IN THE LAND

JOEL 2:12–27

Having brought his listeners to the brink of the Day of the Lord's wrath, Joel pleads with them to repent with sincere hearts. He knows that mere ritual cannot sway the Lord, but he also recognizes the loving and forgiving nature of his God. On that basis he calls for a national assembly of every man, woman, and child in Judah to cry out for mercy. In response, the Lord promises to restore the land to its former state and to bless it anew.

A CALL TO REPENTANCE (2:12–17)

At 2:12 the topic shifts from a threat of judgment to a call for national repentance. First Joel appeals to the gracious nature of the Lord, who might respond favorably to a genuine change of heart. Second, he urges the entire nation to assemble at the temple as one unified body. As we have seen before, Joel marks the boundaries of his topic by an inclusion, repeating the call to cry out and weep before the Lord at both the beginning (v. 12) and end (v. 17) of the section.

Appeal to the Character of the Lord (2:12–14)

Joel's fresh call to repentance builds on the instructions he gave in chapter 1 (esp. vv. 13–14), but some significant differences surface. Previously he dwelled on the element of distress. The people were to show signs of grief and cry out to the Lord, but no direct word was said about "returning" to Him. Now a new climax is reached when Joel calls for a genuine change of heart. He pictures a relentless destruction that builds up even to the consummation of the Day of the Lord. But he says that it is still not too late. Even *now* it is possible for the Lord to show His mercy.

At this point Joel appeals to the covenant that God first made with Israel under Moses. The expression "with all your heart" echoes the first and greatest command to love God above all else (Deut. 6:5), but the phrase also describes how Israel was to obey the law that God gave through Moses (Deut. 10:12; 26:16). In other words, the listeners would understand exactly what the Lord meant when He demanded repentance "with all your heart."

Later in his book Joel makes additional significant references to the Mosaic covenant. At Sinai the people rebelled by making the golden calf. After Moses interceded on their behalf (Deut. 9:25–29), the Lord restated His former promise to send the various seasonal rains, crops of grain, new wine, olive oil, and pasturage for the cattle if the people would obey His commandments (Deut 11:13–15). In like manner, the Lord responded to the efforts of Joel (Joel 2:18–27). Finally, Joel also reminds the Judeans of God's promise to restore the people after they have been scattered among the nations and "return to the Lord your God and obey him with all your heart and with all your soul" (Deut. 30:1–3; see Joel 3:1–8).

Signs of great sorrow and brokenness, such as fasting and mourning, were in order; yet the right perspective was also necessary (2:12–13). The Lord never commanded His people to rend their garments, but sometimes the action accompanied repentance. When Josiah heard the law read, his first action was to tear his clothes (2 Kings 22:11). Later, the prophetess Huldah gave the Lord's response to the king: "Because your heart was responsive and you humbled yourself before the Lord . . . and because you tore your robes and wept in my presence, I have heard you" (22:19; see also 1 Kings 21:27; Ezra 9:3, 5; Jer. 36:24). Since Joel has just spoken of fasting, weeping, and mourning, we should interpret 2:13 as "Rend your heart and not *merely* your garments."

The colorful phrase "rend your heart" is unique to Joel; elsewhere we find instead the concept of coming before God with a "broken" heart (see Ps. 51:17). Of course, Joel does not mean for people literally to tear apart their hearts, but the exaggerated image stresses how urgent the situation is.

The call to repentance bears within it seeds of hope. Having appealed to the people to keep their part of the covenant, Joel focuses on the covenant-keeping God (2:13). Once again he uses traditional language that goes back to Exodus (Ex. 34:6) and Numbers (Num. 14:18), but which also appears in several Psalms (Pss. 86:15; 103:8; 145:8) and in Nehemiah (Neh. 9:17). The closest parallel, however, is Jonah's prayer of complaint after the Assyrians repented (Jonah 4:2). Jonah could not understand why those characteristics of God by which He dealt graciously with Israel should also apply to the Assyrians.

God's "graciousness" meant that He was willing to respond even when His people did not deserve it. The Levites in Nehemiah's time spoke in their prayer of confession about how God had been gracious when the people were stubborn and committed the sin of idolatry (Neh. 9:17). Repentance normally precedes the outpouring of God's grace, but even repentance cannot force action by God because of merit. It is part of His character to show grace in response to genuine repentance. That He went to great lengths to make atonement for sin through the death of His Son is itself an infinite expression of His gracious nature.

When the Scripture writers say that God is "compassionate," they highlight His emotional response. His mercy or compassion flows out of His deep love for His people, who were chosen merely because of His grace. He is eager to forgive, ready to bless.

The Lord is "slow to anger" in that His graciousness makes Him hold back judgment as long as possible. Punishment may be inevitable, but it is God's nature to extend the offer of salvation for the repentant until the last possible moment.

"Love," or "lovingkindness," expresses itself in actions that are merciful and compassionate. The term stresses the Lord's loyalty or faithfulness to His covenant, demonstrated through His willingness to forgive (Ex. 34:6; Num. 14:18; Ps. 86:15). The Lord made an everlasting covenant with His people, Israel. In doing so, He bound Himself by oath (Gen. 22:16–17) to bless the nation. Sometimes the Lord had to punish the people in order to lead them back to His laws. Throughout the history of Israel and Judah the Lord repeatedly exercised His lovingkindness through concrete actions on their behalf.

"He relents from sending calamity" is, in the KJV, "repenteth him of the evil," a translation that could be theologically difficult, especially in light of the way the terms *repent* and *evil* are used in today's English. The underlying Hebrew translated "relent" or "repent" can be used of people who repent from their sins (Job 42:6; Jer. 8:6; 31:19), though the usage is rare. First Samuel 15 uses the term of God in two different ways. Verse 29 says that God, unlike man, does not "change his mind." Yet verse 11 quotes God as saying "I am grieved that I have made Saul king," using the same term. The basic sense of the Hebrew refers to the emotional response to a situation, brought out by "I am grieved." Since emotions often lead to a change in action, the word signifies also the changed behavior that accompanies the emotions involved in repentance. Joel, speaking analogically, refers to God's emotional feeling for His people when they demonstrate repentance that causes Him to turn aside or hold back from a deserved punishment.

The second problematic term, translated *evil* in the KJV (also the NASB), refers to natural catastrophes as well as to moral evil. Thus, it is used of the judgment on Sodom and Gomorrah (Gen. 19:19) and of the Babylonian invasion of Judah (Jer. 1:14). Both incidents were brought about by the Lord, but grounded in His righteous character. In the context of Joel, the thought is that the disaster brought by the locusts could be turned around even while the crisis was going on. More important, the judgment that will come with the Day of the Lord can be turned back. God is not anxious to bring it; He would much prefer to bring a blessing. Hence, it is in His nature to relent or hold back from judgment, even when it is due.[33]

Previously Joel warned that "grain offerings and drink offerings" were cut off from the temple because God brought the locust plague and famine (1:9, 13). In 2:14 he speaks of a possible new harvest from which an offering could be presented. If God chooses to be gracious in response to repentance, says Joel, perhaps there will once again be what is required for the temple service. The renewal of sacrifice will be a sign that the Lord has heard. The Lord restores those who repent so that they can know and serve Him better, not merely so they can be comfortable and prosperous (cf. Eph. 2:10). He knows that it is only as we know Him and serve Him that our spirits find that state of peace or wholeness that the Old Testament refers to as "shalom," particularly in reference to our personal relationship with the living God (see Judg. 6:24; Pss. 4:8; 29:11; 119:165; Isa. 9:6; 26:3; 52:7; Hag. 2:9; Zech. 9:10; also John 14:27; Acts 10:36; Rom. 5:1; Eph. 6:15; Phil. 4:7; Col. 3:15).

Appeal for a Solemn Assembly (2:15–17)

With great urgency Joel exhorts the entire nation to come together for a time of national mourning and appeal to the Lord. All segments of the population are to be present; neither age nor prior responsibility can be exemptions.[34] The priests are to intercede for all the people, calling on the Lord to remember His covenant relationship with them. As the Lord's unique possession, Israel must not be put to shame among the nations.

Only an extreme emergency would make a couple cancel their wedding plans. According to the law of Moses, a man was exempt even from military service for a year after his wedding (Deut. 24:5). Yet not even the anticipated intimacies of the wedding night could excuse the couple from participation in this solemn assembly.

The priests are to stand between the entrance to the temple

and the altar of burnt offering and intercede for the people (2:17). They weep on account of sins. The original Hebrew places some emphasis on their location. Joel wants to be certain that the priests perform the rituals both with a proper attitude of repentance and in the correct manner.

As Joel tells the priests how to pray for the people, he again follows the example of Moses in appealing to the Lord's honor or glory. If Israel had perished while Moses led them in the wilderness, the other nations, which had already been impressed by the deliverance from Egypt, would say that the Lord did not have enough power left to also bring them into Canaan (Num. 14:15–16). Likewise, if Judah, the nation that the Lord claimed as His "inheritance," perishes altogether, then the nations will speak against them in a way that will reflect on the Lord's honor (see Neh. 4:4).

The Lord's Response (2:18–27)

Joel began his book by referring to a story or narrative. Speaking of it at first as simply "anything like this" (1:2), he gradually filled in details of what happened. He asked the people to pass down this story from generation to generation. The story started with the locust plague and it continued with Joel's urgent pleadings for the people to repent. At 2:18 the story continues, told from the standpoint of a narrator describing a past event (see below), with the Lord's response to the people.

However, something seems to be missing from the story. Joel says that *if* the people repent, the Lord *might* respond. Yet now Joel, without telling us that the people *did* repent, seems to say that the Lord *did* respond. The most usual way to translate the Hebrew of 2:18–19 is as follows: "Then the Lord was jealous for his land and took pity on his people, and the Lord replied to them" (basically the NIV with the verbs changed from future to past tense). One way that some Bible versions solve this problem is to translate verse 18 as though it were future: "Then the Lord *will* be jealous for his land and take pity on his people" (NIV, italics added).[35] This seems to solve the problem by extending the description, given in 2:14, of what might happen if the Lord responds to the people. Furthermore, it seems to be supported by the scope of what God will do: "Never again will my people be shamed" (2:26–27; also see v. 19). Surely the destruction of the temple by the Romans in A.D. 70 and the subsequent expulsion of the Jews from their land would seem to belie God's promise.

The most difficult obstacle to this solution is the grammar of the original Hebrew. The verb form used is so well established within all biblical Hebrew literature as a past tense form that it is hard to imagine a future interpretation without strong contextual arguments to the contrary.[36] This is especially true of the introduction to verse 19: "And the Lord answered and said to his people" (author's trans.). It is best to translate 2:18–19a, then, with the past tense.

In his book Joel compares what happened in the past with what will happen in the future. The fact that God responded to His people in the locust plague becomes the pledge that in the future Day of the Lord all who call upon His name will be saved. If the Lord had not responded, who would be present to hear Joel's charge to teach these events to the children and grandchildren (1:3)?

What about the threefold promise: "I will never again make you a reproach among the nations" (2:19, NASB; see also vv. 26–27)? It must be seen within the context of the covenant with Israel, which is eternal. The "reproach" would be if God abandoned His people Israel. The promise God makes through Joel is equivalent to His promise to Abraham and David of an everlasting relationship with Israel. The Jewish people have suffered much, but God has still preserved them from complete destruction. They stand as a testimony to the greatness of our God. Certainly we can also say that the applicability of the promise to individuals within the covenant community depends on individual faith and obedience.[37]

The full sequence of events in the story is as follows: (1) the prophet announces a great catastrophe; (2) he calls for repentance; (3) the people repent; and (4) God responds. That Joel does not report explicitly that the people did repent (#3) calls for some explanation. Of course, when the text says that the

Lord "answered" (v. 19) His people, a response to some action on their part is implied. Still it is unusual that such a major event would only be implied. Would it not be a great thing to report a large-scale response to the preaching of a prophet?

That which is so obvious that it needs no mention is also less important or less prominent. The book of Joel stresses what the Lord does. He brought the locusts and removed them; He will pour out the Spirit and judge the nations. The sovereign God chooses to maintain His eternal covenant with His people not because *they* have responded, but because *He* is gracious and compassionate. Joel's contemporaries must have responded, but the invitation to call upon God and receive His grace remains open forever.

The Lord's response has three parts to it. First (vv. 18–20), the Lord promises to restore the crops and remove the army of locusts. In the second part (vv. 21–23), the people are called to rejoice because the Lord has already begun to act. Evidently fresh rainfall was the sign that the Lord had relented. Finally (vv. 24–27), the Lord promises to make up for what the locusts have done and to live among His people.

How is it that the Lord is "jealous for his land" (2:18)? A key is that, referring to God, Joel speaks of "*his* land" and "*his* people." The Hebrew term designates the strong emotion God feels in His attachment to Israel. It can be translated either "jealous" or "zealous." Here the idea is that the Lord, remembering His everlasting covenant, determined to act swiftly. Isaiah spoke of the Lord's zeal that would fulfill His promises to Israel (Isa. 9:7; 37:32); but the closest parallel is found in Zechariah, who reports God's "gracious" and "comforting" words to His people: "I am very jealous for Jerusalem and Zion" (Zech. 1:14). That is, the Lord has noticed their lowly condition (vision of the myrtle trees, 1:8) but is now prepared to act.

The Lord promises to restore all the yield destroyed by the locusts and to remove the insects far from them. These two actions are linked by a word of reassurance: "And I will never again make you a reproach among the nations" (2:19, NASB).

The promise to drive away "the northern army" (2:20) can

still refer to literal locusts, even though the imagery is military. Jerome observed about a locust plague in his day, "And when the shores of both seas (the Mediterranean and the Dead Sea) were filled with heaps of dead locusts which the waters had cast up, their stench and putrefaction was so noxious as to corrupt the air, so that a pestilence was produced among both beasts and men."[38] Most of Israel's invaders came from the north, because that was the most advantageous way to approach Jerușalem. Since the military language is figurative, it is not necessary to suppose that the locusts also had to come from the north. It would be rare for them to do so, but it would not be without precedent.[39]

The end of verse 20 probably refers to the locusts: "Surely it has acted arrogantly" (author's trans.). Locusts do not have motives, but they have acted like an army that would enter the land and destroy everything at will. The same Hebrew expression is repeated in verse 21 but is there applied to the Lord: "Surely the Lord has done great things." Evidently Joel intends to contrast the arrogant enemy (see Jer. 48:26; Dan. 8:4, 8, 11, 25; Zeph. 2:8, 10) and the Lord (see Ps. 126:2–3).[40]

An alternative view is represented in the NIV, which translates both occurrences of the phrase the same way: "Surely he has done great things." In this view the statement serves as both introduction and conclusion to the reassurance of verse 21, "Be not afraid, O land; be glad and rejoice."

The invitation to rejoice comes first to the ground, then to the animals (2:22), and finally to the people (2:23). Since the people live off the land and the cattle, the whole unit really speaks to the Judeans. Yet when Joel personifies the land and the beasts, it makes the blessing of God seem more vivid. Perhaps the order is intended to replicate that of original creation: earth, beasts, humans. It is as though the Lord re-created Judah after its terrible devastation.

Verse 23 contains one of the most difficult phrases in the book to translate. One of the words in the Hebrew could mean "autumn rains," but "he has given you the autumn rains in righteousness," besides being difficult to understand, also raises a contextual problem. How do we explain the later reference in the same verse to "autumn rains"? The same Hebrew word could also be "teacher" or perhaps even "that which instructs."[41] Then the rain the Lord sends on the earth would be a sign that the Lord has restored a "right" covenant relationship. That is, it "instructs in righteousness." Under this view, the same word would be used with two different meanings, making a play on words: that which instructs in righteousness is, in fact, the autumn rain. Teaching and rain are frequently associated in the Old Testament (1 Kings 8:36; Isa. 30:20–23; 45:8; Hos. 6:3; 10:12). In fact, the pouring out of rain as a sign of righteousness would also parallel the pouring out of the Spirit, which occurs later in Joel (2:28–29). Rain apparently was a sign that the Lord accepted His people's cry for mercy.

Going along with the promise of complete restoration to covenant harmony, the Lord purposes to "repay," or make up for all the damage that the locusts had done (2:25). So He speaks of a great abundance of crops that will completely fill the people's stomachs. What began as mournful sorrow because of emptiness ends with joy because of plenty.

But there are also spiritual blessings. Whereas before the people stood under judgment and the near loss of all hope, now they will praise God's name because of the miracles He has performed. The people will recognize that God is in their midst. Thus, the broken relationship between God and His people will be healed.

Joel sums up God's actions by saying they are "wonders" (2:26–27). The events the prophet has recounted for Judah cannot be explained in any ordinary way. Only the Lord could have brought both the grievous punishment and the joyous relief. Joel tells of these miraculous deeds to cause the people to see the truth: "I [the Lord] am in Israel." For Joel the transformation is complete. Woes have given way to a new glory.

The thrice-repeated promise of no more reproach among the nations is the last thing said in the first half of the book. It points the way forward to God's future dealings with Israel and the nations.

5

WONDERS IN THE EARTH

JOEL 2:28–32

The second half of Joel's book has some important differences from what went before. First, it takes place almost entirely in the future. The only exception is at 3:2–6, which states that the nations will be called to answer before God because of how they have treated His people, Israel, in the past. Here too is a second difference. In the first part of the book we hear nothing about what the nations have done to Israel, only about the damage done by the locusts. Nor is there any word about the destruction of the nations in the first half. Third, the second part of Joel becomes more extravagant about physical and spiritual blessing for Israel when it speaks of the pouring out of the Spirit and of the mountains and hills of Judah flowing with sweet wine and milk.

The final portion of Joel may be divided into two further sections. In the first subsection, Joel speaks of the pouring out of the Spirit and the Day of the Lord (2:28–32). He had already preached that the people must repent in order to escape the judgment of that day. Moreover, historical events had proven him correct. The people repented and the Lord graciously responded, restoring the land and the people. Now it is revealed through Joel that, when the "great and dreadful day of the

Lord" is near, God will pour out His Spirit on all the people of Israel. This will bring about a new era of prophecy, and many will call on the Lord's name and be saved. Joel's successful preaching in his own day foreshadowed this fresh period of prophetic utterance.

In the second subsection, Joel turns to the fate of the nations, including Israel, in the Day of the Lord (3:1–21). God will judge the foreign nations because they have mistreated His people. On the other hand, because Israel is the Lord's special possession, He will save her and pour out His Spirit on her. The nations will be punished according to their guilt. Slave traders will sell the Phoenicians and Philistines to the Judeans; the Lord's army will defeat all the nations in battle; and Egypt and Edom will be left desolate. The Israelites, on the other hand, will return from their captivity and experience unprecedented blessing in their land.

In 2:28–32 Joel talks about the spiritual and physical phenomena of the end times. He looks through the broad sweep of history to the day when the Lord Himself will bring justice to the earth, judging the unrighteous and setting up a new kingdom for His people. As the third chapter of Joel makes clear, all wrongs will be made right in that day. The people will serve God from their hearts and have no reason to fear the terror of God's wrath on the earth.

The Availability of God's Spirit (2:28–29)

After the locust plague, the Lord poured out a blessing of abundant rain to show that He had accepted the repentance of the Judeans (2:18–27). The people were not prepared for the locust invasion, but, when the coming day of God's wrath finally arrives, He will do a fresh spiritual work in them, for repentance is a spiritual change of heart brought about by the Lord. When the people prophesy, it will make the Lord's action in their hearts obvious to all, and He will deliver those who trust in His name. The very elements of the universe will collapse, but God's people will stand firm on their land.

When Joel says, "and afterward" (2:28), he signals to his

readers that he is making new predictions (see Isa. 7:18–23; Hos. 1:5; Amos 9:11; Mic. 5:10; Zeph. 1:10; Zech. 12:3). The previous section also dealt with the future, but those promises were fulfilled, at least in part, when the Lord blessed the land and people after the locust plague. The prophecy of the pouring out of the Spirit, though, looks to a time in Joel's (and, in part, even in our) distant future. Peter quoted Joel 2:28–32 on the day of Pentecost, applying the prophecy to "the last days" (Acts 2:17; see below for further discussion).

Almost immediately Joel centers our attention on the key event of this section, that the Lord pours out His Spirit on "all people." The underlying Hebrew term (lit., "all flesh") can mean all animals and people on earth (Gen. 9:15; Dan. 4:12), but its application is restricted by the context. Since God here speaks of the pouring out of the Spirit, animals are not involved. A more difficult issue is whether the term is restricted only to Israelites (see Jer. 12:12; 45:5; Ezek. 21:4–5) or applies to all people worldwide (Gen. 6:12; Num. 16:22; 27:16; Job 34:15; Ps. 145:21; Zech. 2:13). In two passages it is restricted to all the wicked (Isa. 66:16; Jer. 25:31).

Although this new prophetic word has a certain abruptness, there is no reason to think that Joel does not still address himself to the community of Judah and Jerusalem. Therefore, when he applies the results of the action to his audience ("Your sons . . . your young men"), we should also restrict the action itself to that community. Those who escape the judgment of the Day of the Lord are "on Mount Zion and in Jerusalem." In many other places the Old Testament states that the Lord will pour out His Spirit especially on Israel (Isa. 32:15; 44:3–4; Ezek. 36:27; 37:14; 39:29; Zech. 12:10).[42]

One side of the expression "all flesh" stresses inclusiveness within the sphere intended by the context, but another side sets living creatures apart from God. "All men [flesh] are like grass," proclaims Isaiah, "but the word of our God stands forever" (Isa. 40:6–8). People could not even exist apart from that "breath of God" that gives them life (Gen. 2:7; Job 34:14–15). Yet there will be, says Joel, a new outpouring of God's Spirit that will renew His people.

The image of pouring (referring to a liquid) makes an interesting connection to the promise of rain in 2:23 (see Isa. 44:3). The point is that the Spirit will be available in abundance for anyone in Israel. Though it would still be necessary for individuals to appropriate the gift of God through faith, there is here a special work of God's grace by which He will draw all Israel to Himself (see Zech. 12:10; Rom. 11:25–26).

Joel dwells on one result of God's new presence among His people—prophetic revelation. According to the Hebrew style of expression, this would not exclude other results. Isaiah saw a new era of justice, righteousness, and peace that would accompany the coming of the Spirit (Isa. 32:15–18), whereas Ezekiel pointed to the obedience of those who would be cleansed and given a "new heart" (Ezek. 36:25–27). For Zechariah, the new infusion of the Spirit would give a strong sense of sorrow over the time when the people rejected God's personal representative (the Lord Jesus Christ) among them (Zech. 12:10). All four prophets speak together, however, of a great regathering of God's people to their land (see Joel 3:1). The common time reference leads us to connect these passages even though the prophets saw different (though not conflicting) results.

When Joel speaks of those who prophesy, dream dreams, and see visions, he means that there will be a new era of revelation, with the Israelites preaching to each other. Joel himself is a model for what will happen. He preached repentance, and the whole community responded, with God's blessing coming upon all. In the future, says Joel, the entire population will become prophets, stimulating each other to serve the Lord. God will reveal Himself in this way because of the awesome signs that will accompany the Day of the Lord. Israel will be delivered, and God will use visions and dreams to reassure His people and give a warning to the world.

Most Israelites would have been surprised to think of slaves as participating, in any general way, in an outburst of prophetic visions (2:29). But once large numbers begin to see revelations, the full extent of the miracle will be apparent to all. The text also stresses equal participation in the prophetic activity by women. The Old Testament priesthood was limited to Levite men, and the office of king was hereditary through the son in the line of David. The prophetic office, on the other hand, was always open to anyone, though the number of women who filled the position seems to have been small (see Judg. 5; Ex. 15:20–21; 2 Kings 22:11–20). The New Testament also refers to prophetesses (Luke 2:36). Joel emphasizes that the prophetic gift will be universal among Israelites, even among women and slaves.

The Awesomeness of God's Presence (2:30–31)

The future community will face perils from the coming Day of the Lord similar to the community in Joel's day (2:30). Just as the locusts turned the sky black with their swarms, so the heavens themselves will become even blacker in the coming day. This will be, in fact, "a time of trouble for Jacob" (Jer. 30:4–9). The text does not say exactly how the terrible effects in the sky will happen (2:31). An eclipse could darken the sun, but heavy smoke in the atmosphere may be what turns the moon to blood-red. Perhaps the smoke will derive from volcanic and tectonic activity on the earth as well as through war (see Zech. 12:2–9; 14:1–5).[43]

David Allan Hubbard notes three purposes of the smoke in this passage. First, "it reminds us of the deeds of God in the Exodus" (Ex. 19:18). Second, "it conveys the sights and smells of battle, as the Lord wages war against his enemies" (Isa. 34:5–10; Ezek. 32:7–15; 38:22). Third, "it pictures God's judgment as a worldwide sacrifice to his holiness" (Isa. 34:6, 10).[44]

A "wonder" points to the power of God who is able to bring it about, causing amazement and awe (see Ex. 4:21; 1 Kings 13:3, 5; 2 Chron. 32:24; Zech. 3:8). The signs will spread dread and fear as they anticipate the moment of the Lord's arrival on earth to carry out His judgment. These signs are similar to those of Revelation 6:12–17, which make the people say to the mountains and rocks, "Fall on us and hide us from the face of him who sits on the throne and from the wrath of the Lamb! For the great day of their wrath has come, and who can stand?" (Rev. 6:16–17)

The signs in heaven and earth immediately precede the Day of the Lord proper. This is because the main event of that day will be when the Lord Himself appears on the earth (see Zech. 14:4). Then in His wrath He will judge the nations, which have mistreated His people (see Zeph. 1:18, "the day of the Lord's wrath"), but deliver all who call upon Him. Depending on the context, "day of the Lord" may include the broader period of the Lord's visitation, which culminates in the setting up of His kingdom on earth (Zech. 14), or it may stress (as in Joel) the central event of His actual appearance on earth to judge the nations.

The Availability of God's Salvation (2:32)

Just as the people in Joel's day called on the Lord and were saved, so none need perish in the Day of the Lord (2:32). As long as Israel is in a state of apostasy from her God, she stands under the fear of His wrath. But Joel speaks of a God who is so gracious that He sends His Spirit to prepare His chosen people, turning them back to Him so they can receive a blessing rather than judgment.

The term "survivors" might imply that only those Israelites who turn back to the Lord will escape His wrath (see Gen. 32:8; 2 Kings 19:31; Ezra 9:13; Neh. 1:2). From the community that returns to the land, however, individuals will come to the Lord in unprecedented numbers because of the action of the Spirit.

Those delivered will "call on" the Lord, but the Lord "calls" the survivors. The verse reinforces the opening remarks about the gift of the Spirit. God's grace made it possible for Israel not only to obtain deliverance, but also to repent. Everything is ultimately wrapped up in His gracious election of His people (see 2:13; Eph. 2:8–9).

The structure of 2:32 is as follows:

1. Statement of deliverance—freely available for all who call on the name of the Lord
2. Reason for deliverance—a previous promise of the Lord
3. Further assurance of deliverance—the Lord will call out the survivors

Excursus

Because it is a subject of much contemporary relevance to the church, I will discuss in more detail Peter's quotation of Joel on the day of Pentecost. After denying that the Christians were drunk, Peter declared: "This is what was spoken by the prophet Joel" (Acts 2:16). Peter had no hesitation about connecting the two texts, but numerous questions arise because the passages do not completely overlap in their contextual meaning.

The differences seem obvious enough. Joel speaks of dreams and visions, whereas the Christians experienced the ability to speak in different languages. The sun did not darken at Pentecost, nor did the moon turn to blood; and the Lord did not appear with wrath against the nations.

There are also some significant similarities between the two passages. First, in each case the Lord pours out the Holy Spirit on the community of regathered Israel. At Pentecost Jews were present from all over the Greco–Roman world. Note also that Peter goes on to say that after Jesus rose from the dead and was exalted to the Father's right hand, He "poured out what you now see and hear" (Acts 2:33). "Pour out" comes from the same word used in the Greek translation (Septuagint) of Joel 2:28–29.

Also, though Joel gives a prominence to prophetic activity that goes beyond the things happening in Peter's day, the New Testament came into existence in the first century through a new burst of revelation, and Luke stressed various prophetic activities in the early Christian community. Peter's sermon itself contained new revelation and was in fact a prophecy. The church community then united around the "apostles' teaching" (Acts 2:42). Peter continued to preach prophetic sermons (Acts 3:12–26; 10:34–43), and Stephen (Acts 7) and Paul (Acts 17:22–31) made their own contributions. The latter two also had visions of the risen Christ (Acts 7:55–56; 9:3–6), and Peter saw a vision and heard the Spirit direct him to Cornelius (Acts 10:9–20). Even Cornelius saw an angel who told him to send men to Peter (Acts 10:1–7). Similar incidents abound in the book of Acts (8:26–40; 12:7–10; 13:2, 9–11; 16:6–10; 21:10–11).

Another item of interest is the miraculous signs and wonders of Pentecost, even though they are not the same ones mentioned by Joel. Peter stressed that God had performed "miracles, wonders and signs" through Jesus while He was present on earth (Acts 2:22), "wonders and signs" being the same words Peter cited from Joel's prophecy. At least some of these signs were astronomical (Luke 23:44–45). The miracle of tongues was also a sign, and Luke continues to mention throughout the book of Acts various wonders and signs performed by Christians through the power of God (see Acts 10:44–48).

Also, Peter's use of "last days" in his citation of Joel links the prophecy and the events of Pentecost. The New Testament writers thought of the "last days" in two ways. On the one hand, it included both comings of Christ, in that the appearance of Jesus Christ on earth has such overwhelming significance to the program of God for both Israel and the church (Heb. 1:2; compare 2 Tim. 3:1). In this sense, Peter seems to make the link between Joel's prediction and the day of Pentecost. Peter recognized that something dramatically new was beginning, and that God's work among people would never be the same again. On the other hand, the New Testament writers also recognize that the "last days" will be the time when the work that God has already begun will culminate in the return of Christ to the earth for judgment (James 5:3; 2 Peter 3:3). That is also the time that the Old Testament prophets seem to associate with a fresh work of the Holy Spirit of unprecedented magnitude.

What about the wrath that God will pour out on the nations? It is instructive to notice that both the Joel passage and Peter's sermon are written to encourage the listeners; God's wrath need not be directed at them. All that is necessary is to repent and call on the name of the Lord (see Acts 2:38). Peter did not know when the time of wrath would come, nor did Joel state precisely how much time would elapse between the coming of the Spirit and "the great and awesome day of the Lord" (Joel 2:31, NASB).

Finally, how do the Gentiles fit into God's plan? In the book of Acts, Luke shows the readers how it was only with great reluctance that the early church, including Peter, concluded that salvation was for the Gentiles also. Therefore, it seems unlikely that Peter used the Joel passage to teach that "all flesh" extended to the Gentiles. Some have noted that he applied the "promise" to "all who are far off" (Acts 2:39) and concluded that this refers to the Gentiles.[45] More likely it refers to those Jews who were unable to get to Jerusalem for Pentecost, or possibly to distant generations of Jews (i.e., "their children to the next generation," see Joel 1:3).

That the Gentiles did receive the Spirit at a later time has a simple explanation. While Joel preached to the Jews, he does not suggest that it was impossible for the Gentiles to obtain the same deliverance. The extension of the promise of the Spirit to Gentiles was something new, but it was not inconsistent with Joel's vision. As Paul would explain later, the Gentiles were like a wild olive branch grafted into the cultivated olive tree which represents God's chosen people (Rom. 11:17). God's purposes for Israel will yet be accomplished. In the meantime, the Gentiles enjoy the blessings of the age of grace.

The Old Testament clearly makes room for the Gentiles in the plan of God. This is especially true of the promise to Abraham: "and all peoples on earth will be blessed through you" (Gen. 12:3). Exactly how the Gentiles would participate in the promises of God remained a mystery until it was revealed to the New Testament writers.

Comparison demonstrates, then, considerable overlap between Joel's prediction that God would pour out His Spirit on "all flesh" and the situation of the church at Pentecost and its early stages of growth. Actually, we might say that the latter events are a fulfillment "in miniature" of Joel's prophecy. The astronomical signs that accompanied the first coming of Christ will be intensified at the Second Coming. The Jews who gathered from around the world to Jerusalem on Pentecost were but a small portion of the great and permanent return that will take place in the future. Finally, the Spirit will bring about the repentance of all Israel before the final Day of the Lord. Though large numbers of Jews responded to Peter's call for repentance at Pentecost, the book of Acts demonstrates the increasing rejection of

Christ by the Jews and the simultaneous offer of salvation to the Gentiles.

Walter Kaiser makes an important statement about the problem:

> We conclude that the promise of the outpouring of the Holy Spirit in the last days has received a preliminary fulfillment in the series of events at Pentecost, Samaria, and Caesarea. But those events and the subsequent baptisms of the Holy Spirit that take place whenever anyone receives Christ as Lord and Savior and is thereby ushered into the family of God are all mere harbingers and samples of that final downpour that will come in that complex of events connected with Christ's second return. However, these events—past, present, and future—make up one generic whole concept, for in the prophet's view there is a wholeness and a totality to what he sees.[46]

To this I would add that the Lord gave Peter new insight when He took the event Joel foresaw and linked it with the onset of the new age of the Spirit. In other words, Joel saw the end point of the whole process, while Peter fixed his eyes on the beginning.

What is the implication of Peter's reference to Joel's prophecy for the relationship between Israel and the church? If one assumes a literal fulfillment for the many prophecies concerning national Israel, it will not do to say only that the church is spiritual Israel. On the other hand, some stress the discontinuity to the point that the events of Pentecost cannot have any direct relationship to Joel's prophecy. A note in the *New Scofield* on Joel 2:28 says, for example, "Peter quoted Joel's prediction as an illustration of what was taking place in his day, and as a guarantee that God would yet completely fulfill all that Joel had prophesied." Charles Feinberg notes the lack of "the customary formula for a fulfilled prophecy" in Acts 2:16 in support of this interpretation.[47] To this latter argument Walter Kaiser responds, "The truth of the matter is that there is no single [fulfillment] formula used consistently in Acts or elsewhere in the NT for that matter."[48]

Robert Chisholm argues that "in the early chapters of Acts the kingdom was being offered to Israel once more." Thus, Peter thought that "the outpouring of the Holy Spirit signaled the coming of the Millennium. However, the complete fulfillment of the prophecy (with respect to both the extent of the Spirit's work and the other details) was delayed because of Jewish unbelief. . . ."[49] This idea has some strengths, especially in that it permits fulfillment in some sense *both* at Pentecost and in the Millennium. However, in our view more allowance needs to be made for the fact that Pentecost represents the inception of the church. Thus, something more foundational must have happened than simply an offer which was "delayed because of Jewish unbelief."

Paul's analogy of the vine with Gentiles grafted in can be helpful here. The work of Christ at His first coming is just as foundational to the future work of God in national Israel as to His present work with the church. The same is true for Jesus Christ's pouring out of the Spirit from heaven (Acts 2:33). There is one people of God, but the Lord's special dealings with the church now and with national Israel in the future represent different phases or emphases in His overall plan.[50]

Perhaps Pentecost can be called the time of first fruits. It was the inauguration of the age of the Spirit. Joel's prophecy can apply throughout the "last days." There is no inherent reason to restrict his statement about the gift of the Spirit to one particular occasion.[51] When the Lord regathers Israel for the final time there may be more than one occasion for the Spirit to be poured out upon God's people, as we may imply from the variety of other Old Testament references to the event. The New Testament reveals additionally that the "last days" will extend throughout the Church age, and that the Gentiles can enjoy the spiritual benefits previously reserved for Israel through the outpouring of the Spirit.[52]

Finally, a practical question arises concerning this discussion. To what extent should Christians at the present time expect to participate in prophecy, whether through dreams or visions? First, while there was a great outburst of prophetic activity in the New Testament period, it should be remembered that the New Testament has rendered the revelatory function of the prophet unnecessary. Scripture is now complete (the foundational work of the apostles and prophets, Eph. 2:20; compare Rev. 22:18–19), and God's revelation in Christ is final (Heb. 1:1–3). Second, Christian leaders, such as pastors and teachers, sometimes have functions like those of a prophet: to critique the church in light of the Bible; to focus attention on God's work in current history, also in light of Scripture; and to intercede in prayer for the people. Third, the Holy Spirit illuminates all believers, helping them to understand the Bible and to have insight into how to apply it to themselves and to others to whom they minister. That is our "foretaste" of the greater prophetic outbursts that lie in the time after the church has been raptured. Fourth, there are false prophets as well as true, so believers must be cautious about believing claims to new prophetic revelation. No true prophet would ever lead people away from God and what He says in His Word (Deut. 13:1–5). Nor would a true prophet ever make predictions that do not come true (Deut. 18:20–22).

6

JUDGMENT IN THE EARTH

JOEL 3:1–21

Joel turns in the last chapter of his book to the Lord's final judgment of the nations. The time of this judgment continues to be that "great and dreadful day of the Lord." God will yet pour out His wrath on the nations, but He will restore Israel to her former glory and pour out blessings on her such as she has never known.

Joel 3 has four parts, arranged in a parallel pattern. The first and third sections deal in a general way with judgment of the nations as well as the deliverance and restoration of Israel. In the second and fourth sections, however, Joel singles out specific nations, and their punishment consists of how they are made to submit to Israel. That is, they either become slaves to Israel, or their land becomes a desolation in contrast to the renewal of the land of Judah.

THE LORD JUDGES THE NATIONS FOR THEIR TREATMENT OF ISRAEL (3:1–3)

Chapter 3 begins with a prophecy; the Lord will restore Judah and Jerusalem but gather the nations for judgment in "the Valley of Jehoshaphat." The Lord summons them there because they treated His chosen people like slaves, scattering them throughout the earth.

It is clear from 3:1 that the Lord will restore Judah and Jerusalem when He judges the nations. The idiom "restore the fortunes of" often refers to the Millennium (see Ps. 14:7; Ezek. 39:25; Amos 9:14; Zeph. 3:20), though some instances are found in a purely historical context (Ps. 126:1; Lam. 2:14; Ezek. 29:14).

According to 3:2, the nations will be judged in a broad plain. No one knows where the "Valley of Jehoshaphat" is. Actually, the name is symbolic, stressing what happens there rather than where it is. "Jehoshaphat" means "the Lord [Yahweh] judges," and the verse continues, "There I will enter into judgment against them." The play on words is clear in the original Hebrew as well as in the English "judge"/"judgment." Later (3:14), Joel refers to the place as the valley of "decision." Possibly "Jehoshaphat" was intended to call to mind the time when God defeated the Ammonites, Moabites, and Edomites on behalf of Jehoshaphat, king of Judah (2 Chron. 20), though the text need not imply that the judgment will happen at the same place. Zechariah mentions a "great valley" formed when the Lord's feet touch the Mount of Olives (14:4), but the main purpose of that valley is for the Jews to escape from the nations. Of course, judgment could occur there once the Lord's people have fled.[53]

All the nations will be judged at Jehoshaphat Valley, indicating that they are all guilty of crimes against Israel. Specifically, they "scattered" her among the nations. If Joel lived during the preexilic period, then the only specific instances of scattering would include certain raids against the southern kingdom. During the reign of Rehoboam, the Egyptian Pharaoh Shishak carried away much plunder, though the Bible says nothing of captives (1 Kings 14:25–26; 2 Chron. 12:2–6). Later the Philistines and Arabs conducted a raid against Judah, taking treasure and captives from the royal house of Jehoram (2 Chron. 21:16–17).

Sennacherib was the first Assyrian king to trouble Judah, but he was unable to take Jerusalem. Hezekiah gave him tribute from his own palace and from the temple (2 Kings 18:14–16), but again no mention is made of captives. Sennacherib himself boasted of carrying away 200,150 people from the other towns of Judah and various women from Hezekiah's court.[54] Whether this boast is accurate is hard to say. Next we hear of the Assyrians carrying away Manasseh to Babylon in chains (2 Chron. 33:11). Probably other prisoners were taken at the same time.

When Jerusalem fell in 586 B.C., the Babylonians deported a great part of the population to various parts of the empire. It is also clear that other nations participated in the downfall of the Judean kingdom (see 2 Kings 24:2; Ezek. 25:2–3, 8, 12, 15–17; 26:2; Obad. 10–14). Soon after, a group of Judeans emigrated to Egypt (Jer. 43:4–7). Some Judeans returned to the land when Cyrus of Persia issued his decree in 538 B.C. (2 Chron. 36:22–23; Ezra 1:1–4), but many remained in their exile. During the reign of Xerxes (Ahasuerus, 486–465 B.C.), the Jews were still "dispersed and scattered among the peoples in all the provinces" of the Persian empire (Est. 3:8).

No activity against Judah prior to the fall of Jerusalem fits easily with Joel's talk about the nations dispersing the population, dividing up the land, and selling some of the people into slavery. From a prophetic perspective, these events could still lie within Joel's future. Keil, for example, thought that some of the events of verses 2–3 could only have taken place under the Romans.[55]

It seems most natural here to interpret the destruction of Jerusalem as an event in Joel's past. If Babylon has already fallen, it would be possible for him to pass by that nation and dwell more particularly on nations that remain to be judged (vv. 4, 19). In any case, the wrath of the Lord will be poured out on all nations specifically because of the way they have treated Israel, His own possession (see Matt. 25:31–46). The events surrounding the Babylonian capture of Jerusalem become a paradigm, as it were, for the way nations throughout history have treated Israel. As Feinberg so aptly states, "Little do the nations realize how they incur the wrath of God when they lay violent hands upon His heritage and the plant of His choosing."[56]

The Babylonians did not bring new people into Judah to inhabit it. They incorporated the territory into the Babylonian empire. This may be what Joel means when he says the nations "divided up my land" (3:2). Or he may mean that Israel's neighbors, especially Tyre, Sidon, and Philistia (see 3:4–8), divided up the territory among themselves.[57]

The language of the passage grows out of the very personal relationship between the Lord and His people. When He calls them "my inheritance" (3:2), He refers to the process of distributing the land as it was set up in the days of Moses and Joshua and continued in the institution of the year of Jubilee (Lev. 25:8–55). God, according to the Old Testament, owns the entire earth because He created it, but Israel is His special possession. Imagine then how serious the charge is against the nations: They took the Lord's very own possession and divided it up for themselves.

Imagine the chaos after invaders have penetrated a great city. The soldiers are prone to mob action and atrocities (v. 3). They kill all the defending warriors, but capture the defenseless for their own uses. They throw dice to decide who gets the best women and the strongest slaves. A man sees a woman he wants and trades a mere boy for her. Another wants wine and gives a young girl for it. These are commonplaces of war (Obad. 13–14; Zech. 14:2), yet the Lord does not consider them any less abhorrent because of this fact. The nations will have to answer directly to God for having treated His own personal possession, the "apple of his eye" (Zech. 2:8), so lightly.

The Lord Punishes Tyre, Sidon, and Philistia (3:4–8)

The Lord singles out Phoenicia and Philistia for special punishment because they tried to remove the Judeans far from their territory. The Lord will reverse the situation, enabling Judah and Jerusalem to sell the Phoenicians and Philistines to the Sabeans, a nation far away.

The Lord asks a rhetorical question of Israel's neighbors (3:4). The question implies that the Lord knows how important these nations feel, but He also knows how insignificant they really are. We might paraphrase, "You are of no special importance to Me." These willful nations actually thought they could escape the same punishment reserved for all the rest of the nations.[58]

Various nearby nations helped plunder Judah when the Babylonians conquered it, leading the reader to wonder, *Why single out Tyre, Sidon, and Philistia?* Perhaps these nations were excessively bold in their hostility toward the Lord and His people. They were intimately involved with the trading of Hebrew slaves, as the following verse (3:6) makes plain.[59] Or, according to Hebrew style, Tyre, Sidon, and Philistia may represent the nations in general. Tyre and Sidon belong together (Phoenicia), and with the Philistine plain practically the entire coastland in the vicinity of Israel is represented. Edom and Egypt also get special mention near the end of the chapter (3:19).

Evidently the Phoenicians and Philistines took some action to try to "pay back" the Lord for something He did (3:4). It is not clear whether a hostile or friendly action is meant. On the one hand, it may be that these nations think their actions against Israel are somehow going to do the Lord a favor, but the Lord interprets it as hostile because of Judah's involvement. On the other hand, the thought may be: "Do you think mistreating My people this way will get back at Me for past victories they have had over you?"[60] The Lord is more powerful than the arrogant nations. He will respond swiftly and thoroughly. The very crimes they have committed will boomerang on them (see Ps. 7:16; Obad. 15).

The plunder the nations took was the Lord's ("my silver and my gold," 3:5) because Judah was His personal possession (3:2). The nations despoiled the Judeans and used the treasures for their own pleasure.

The Greeks appear in 3:6 as a people so far away from Judah that the slave dealers who sold to them would not think of the captives as ever being able to return. Ezekiel 27:13 mentions the trade relations between Phoenicia and Greece ("Javan" in some versions). How appropriately the punishment fits the crime! From the very places these slave traders have driven away God's people (3:7), the Lord will stir them up and bring them back to do the same thing to their enemies.

Unless we are to assume that enslavement to another nation would be a condition of the Millennium, the fulfillment of the punishment should be sought in history. Yet historical information about such a sale is scanty. Allen mentions that Antiochus III sold the Sidonians into slavery in 345 B.C. and that Alexander the Great enslaved Tyre and Gaza in 332 B.C.[61] Possibly Jews purchased some of the slaves and then resold them to the Sabeans, though this is only speculation.

Chisholm argues that the historical fulfillment "prefigures" the passage's "eschatological significance." That is, "Philistia and Phoenicia represent all of Israel's enemies (much as do Moab in Isa. 25:10–12 and Edom in the book of Obadiah). At that time God's people will gain ascendancy over their foes (see Isa. 41:11–12; Amos 9:12; Obad. 15–21; Mic. 7:16–17; Zeph. 2:6–7)."[62] Since the chapter apparently falls within the scope of "the latter days," there is some point to Chisholm's view. Yet we would still maintain that a strictly literal fulfillment of the prophecy that Judeans will sell their former enemies into slavery to another nation must occur prior to the Millennium (and perhaps has already occurred).

Actually, it may be that Joel digresses in 3:4–8 from the main issue of the Day of the Lord to a special word of judgment which will not necessarily be fulfilled in the "latter days." In any case, Joel focuses a lot of attention on these verses. He changes his style from poetry to prose; he gives more detail about the guilt of the nations first mentioned in 3:2; he concentrates the various parties involved, mentioning Tyre, Sidon, Philistia, the Greeks, the Sabeans, and the Judeans; and he gives the sense of being in a courtroom, with God examining the nations. Joel apparently wanted to deal with an incident still fresh in the minds of his audience. The people of Judah had strong feelings about what the Phoenicians and Philistines did to them, and the Lord seeks to reassure His people that justice will be done.

THE LORD DEFEATS THE NATIONS BUT DELIVERS ISRAEL (3:9-17)

Joel resumes the theme of judgment in the Valley of Jehoshaphat in 3:9–17. With language that reminds us of Joel's plea for the Judeans to assemble at the temple to fast and pray, the nations are summoned to the valley for a battle. But when they arrive, they will find the Lord waiting to judge them like a farmer commanding his servants to reap the harvest. Intense darkness will cover the earth at this time, but the Lord will save His people Israel.

A cry for war goes out among the nations (3:9). Addressing no one nation in particular, Joel gives the commands, "Prepare for war! Rouse the warriors!" This informs the readers that God will stir up the nations to war (see Obad. 1; Hag. 2:21). There is a close parallel in structure between this verse and the time when Joel called the people of Judah to come to the temple to pray and fast (Joel 1:13–14; 2:15–16). When the Judeans heeded that call, the Lord relented from the judgment and healed the land.

Now a call goes out to the nations. They are to come to Jehoshaphat Valley to do battle, where they will be destroyed by the full fury of God's wrath. A certain irony in the wording of the summons highlights the contrast. The Judeans came together for repentance and were delivered. The nations come together for war with God and are destroyed.

The expression "prepare for war" (3:9) is literally something like "sanctify a war." It is the same term Joel used in 2:15, "Declare a holy fast." Applied to warfare, the term implies that the enemies offer sacrifices or make other types of religious preparations when they muster the troops.[63] Allen recognizes the irony of calling the nations to a holy war that will lead to their own defeat by the Lord.[64] In the parallel structures of 1:14 (and 2:15) and 3:9 the "warriors" correspond to the "elders," while "all the fighting men" echoes "all who live in the land." The latter expression is expanded in 2:16 to the various categories of people who live in the land (e.g., "children").

Isaiah (2:4) and Micah (4:3) both predict that the nations will "beat their swords into plowshares and their spears into pruning hooks." How do we account for the contrast with Joel's statement in 3:10? Does he contradict these other prophets? Or do they contradict him? They have different perspectives. Joel envisions the judgment that will take place *before* the messianic kingdom is set up. Isaiah and Micah, on the other hand, view what happens *after* "the mountain of the Lord's temple" is established "as the chief among the mountains." Then the survivors of the nations that remain will go up to Jerusalem to worship the Lord, learning peace instead of war.

Joel may have quoted a popular saying often used when preparing for war. The other prophets then changed its common meaning to suit a different context. Or Joel might have adapted it from Isaiah and Micah, especially considering the way he frames his appeal to the nations to sound like a summons from the Lord.

It is unusual that Joel interjects a prayer into his speech to the nations, "Bring down your warriors, O Lord!" This adds to the urgency of the message. Also, the similarities we have seen with Joel 2:16–17 might help to explain the presence of a prayer. In the earlier passage Joel gave a prayer for the priests to say, prefaced by "Spare your people, O Lord."

The "warriors" Joel calls for in his prayer must be the angelic hosts who assist God in the judgment (see Ps. 103:20; Zech. 14:5). The term fits the context of a battle scene well, though it does not elsewhere refer to angels. It is, though, the same term used for "warriors" in 3:9. The nations bring their warriors, and the Lord will bring His army down from heaven.

According to 3:12, the Lord sits to hold court, a scene similar to that of Daniel 7:9–14 and of Matthew 25:31–46 (see also Matt. 24:29–31). The scene is central to the structure of the section. First, Joel issued the commands to the nations (3:9–12a). In 3:13 the Lord issues instructions to His angelic attendants. In the center of the action sits the Lord Himself, ready to decide the verdict.

The scene changes from one of war to harvest. The ripe crops, along with the full wine press and overflowing vats, indicate that the nations are ready for judgment (see Jer. 51:33; Hos. 6:11; Amos 8:1). At last their wickedness is complete, and God must act. The commands in this verse, plural in form, are probably given to the "warriors" (v. 11). The New Testament also teaches that God's angels will participate in a harvest of judgment (Matt. 24:31; Rev. 14:14–20).

There is a clear connection between the harvest of judgment and the agricultural imagery of the first part of Joel. The locusts and drought prevented any harvesting, but later God promised a renewed harvest of plenty after His people repented. For the nations, the harvest time means that they are ripe for judgment.

"Jehoshaphat" contains within it the Hebrew word for "judge," and the term "decision" (3:14) can mean to render a judgment (1 Kings 20:40). Thus the meaning "verdict" or "decision" fits the context well. However, the noun can also mean that which is dug out or excavated ("trench" in Dan. 9:25). Aside from the legal context, then, the phrase might mean something like "a deep valley."

The nations are packed so tightly into the valley that they jostle each other and shout loudly. Not only do the peoples overflow with wickedness; their sheer numbers fill up the large area set aside by God to render their verdict. "Tumults" seems a better translation than the traditional "multitudes," because the original Hebrew implies the noise as well as the size.

In 3:14 Joel repeats one of his motifs, "the day of the Lord is near." Here the closeness of that day is virtually equivalent to its actual presence. The final moment toward which Joel has been building throughout the book has finally arrived.

The sun, moon, and stars become dark with the coming of the Day of the Lord, and heaven and earth shake (3:15–16). These are the same cosmic signs that accompanied the locusts (2:10), though they are on a much more universal scale. All these ominous events take place as the Lord Himself speaks His judgment from Zion and Jerusalem. The wicked will not be able to flee from the presence of the Lord seated on His throne. This judgment is to be distinguished from that held before "the great white throne," which will take place after the Millennium (Rev. 20:4–15).

The act of judgment itself is represented by a terrible roar, like that of a lion, issuing from the Lord's mouth. The same statement is found in Amos 1:2, where it applies to judgment on the northern kingdom of Israel. For Joel the Lord's roar reflects His earlier commands to His army of locusts (2:11).

A great earthquake follows the roar, shaking the whole

earth to its foundations and setting even the heavens tottering (see Zech. 14:4–5). Just as none could have endured the army of locusts unless the Lord had poured out His grace, so all people on earth stand in danger from the appearance of God on Zion.

Only in the Lord Himself, who is "gracious and compassionate, slow to anger and abounding in love, and he relents from sending calamity" (2:13), can His people escape from wrath. Those who have called on His name will discover that nothing can harm them when they are under His protection.

God completes His act of grace when He reaffirms His covenant with His people (3:17). The locusts and drought threatened that relationship in Joel's day. At the brink of extinction, the people threw themselves on the mercy of the Lord. He relented and restored their land; then He confirmed His position as Israel's God (2:27).

The same cycle will recur in the future. The time when the Lord pours out His wrath, coming on the heels of the time of Jacob's trouble, will appear to overwhelm the whole earth. But God will pour out His Spirit, motivating the elect to call on His name. Then all Israel will be saved and recognize their unique relationship to the Lord once again.

For thousands of years the Jews have heard the tramping of foreign boots through their holy city. The "angel of the Lord" kept out the Assyrians (Isa. 37:36–37), but later the Babylonian army marched in (2 Kings 25:1–17). When the exiles returned, they discovered strangers who frustrated their efforts to rebuild the temple (Ezra 4). Throughout the coming years Greeks, Romans, Arabs, and Crusaders invaded the city. What a welcome sound to Jewish ears—"never again will foreigners invade her" (3:17).

Other prophets speak of a time when the nations will go up to Jerusalem to learn the ways of the Lord (Isa. 2:2–4; Mic. 4:1–4). Joel does not mean to deny this. He speaks of foreigners, whereas Isaiah and Micah speak of those who *learn* the ways of the Lord. They no longer have aspirations to seize the land; they become more like sojourners than foreigners.

We call Jerusalem "the Holy City," but she will not really be holy again until God dwells within her. Then, as the prophet

Zechariah puts it,

> On that day *holy to the Lord* will be inscribed on the bells of the horses, and the cooking pots in the Lord's house will be like the sacred bowls in front of the altar. Every pot in Jerusalem and Judah will be holy to the Lord Almighty, and all who come to sacrifice will take some of the pots and cook in them. (Zechariah 14:20–21)

The holiness of God's presence will pervade everything and every person within the walls of the city.

Zechariah goes on to predict that the "Canaanite" or "merchant" will no longer be in God's house in those days.[65] The thought is very close to Joel's remark about foreigners. Just as merchants had no place in the sacred precincts of the temple (compare how Jesus drove the money changers out of the temple), so those with the impure motive of conquest will have no part in the sacred city.

The Lord Blesses Judah but Makes Egypt and Edom Desolate (3:18–21)

The conclusion to the second half of Joel centers around the unprecedented blessing in the land of Judah that will accompany the millennial kingdom. Egypt and Edom enter the scene only as a contrasting background. The utter desolation of their land makes Judah's fruitfulness stand out more boldly.

This section corresponds to the conclusion of the first half of the book, which speaks of a restoration in extra measure for the devastation caused by the locust plague. According to both parts, the Lord will restore His close relationship with His people as He dwells in Zion. Yet in the millennial kingdom the blessings will be unusual in scope, and the Lord will make Judah and Jerusalem a home for them forever.

The Hebrew prophets used the phrase "[and it will happen] in that day" to mark off a new section, as here in 3:18. As is so often the case in predictive portions of the Old Testament, "that day" refers to the general events surrounding the Day of the Lord. Judgment of the nations and deliverance for Israel do not exhaust God's purposes. He has planned a new blessing for the land that will surpass even the splendor of the kingdoms of David and Solomon.

The covenant with Israel included a promise of land. That is why the prophets were so often concerned about the condition of the ground. Would it be productive or desolate? Who would own it? God reassured His people after He destroyed the locusts that the ruined land would once again overflow with wine, oil, and grain. Now Joel returns to the same theme, but with much more extravagant language.

Everything will grow in such abundance that the mountains will appear to have springs of wine dripping from them. The cattle will be so well fed (see Joel 1:18) that the excess milk will pour down the hillsides into the valleys. Perhaps the extravagant language reflects also Jacob's blessing for Judah in Genesis 49:11–12.[66] All of this will be made possible by a plenteous supply of water for the thirsty ground. It will even flow out from the house of God in Jerusalem itself (see Ezek. 47:1–12; Zech. 14:8).

Since the lower stretch of the Kidron Valley would be the natural destination for all water flowing from the temple area, the "valley of acacias" should probably be located there.[67] The word for "valley" refers to a dry streambed that has water only during the rainy season. By extension it also can refer to the depression that has been carved out by the rapidly flowing water. By a creative miracle the Lord will make a ceaseless spring of water flow out so that the usually dry area will be constantly wet. "Shittim," found in some versions (e.g., the NASB), is the Hebrew term for acacia trees, evergreens with yellow flowers and useful wood that grow mainly in the valleys around the Dead Sea.[68]

Egypt and Edom, mentioned in 3:19, highlight Judah's fruitfulness by way of contrast. The Nile overflows regularly and makes the land along its banks lush and fertile, but the judgment at the "valley of decision" will reduce it to a wasteland. Writing with reference to the time after the Millennium has begun, Zechariah also singled out Egypt. She will especially suffer God's plague of no rainfall if the Egyptians refuse to go to

Jerusalem to celebrate the Feast of Tabernacles (Zech. 14:18–19).

Perhaps Edom receives special mention because her people descended from Esau, Jacob's brother. There should have been a closeness between the two; instead there was perpetual hatred (see Amos 1:11–12; Obad. 10). Edom will also become a desolate wilderness, dry and lifeless in comparison with well-watered Judah.

The indictment of violence against Judah applies to both Egypt and Edom, but especially to Edom. Obadiah 10 refers to "the violence against your brother Jacob." The Edomites committed their worst crime against Judah when they betrayed their brother-nation during the Babylonian conquest (see discussion of Obad. 10–14). The most notable example of Egyptian violence was when Pharaoh Neco killed King Josiah at Megiddo (2 Kings 23:29). There were other occasions when Egypt either invaded Judah (1 Kings 14:25–26) or proved to be a false ally (Isa. 36:6; Jer. 2:36; Ezek. 29:6–7).

When God establishes His kingdom, none will ever destroy it (3:20; see also Dan. 7:27). At this time the Lord Jesus Christ will sit on His throne to fulfill the promise to David of an everlasting dynasty (2 Sam. 7:13; Rev. 20:4).

It is difficult to interpret the first part of 3:21. The NIV takes the Hebrew expression "their blood" to mean bloodguiltiness that Israel had incurred: "Their bloodguilt, which I have not pardoned, I will pardon." Yet it is hard to see from the context why or how Israel should have this guilt. Allen ingeniously suggests the line be rendered as a question: "And shall I leave their bloodshed unpardoned? I shall not leave (it) unpardoned."[69] However, it does not seem possible to interpret the original this way.

A better translation might be, "Thus I will avenge their blood which I have not avenged." This rendering follows the ancient versions and the NASB (see also JB). To paraphrase, "And after I have judged the nations I will be free from my obligation concerning the blood of Judah."[70]

In a final outburst of faith Joel proclaims, "The Lord dwells in Zion!" (3:21) Judah was threatened by a locust plague, but the Lord was gracious and restored His nation. The inhabitants were scattered to the far corners of the earth and were roughly treated at the hands of the Gentiles. Yet the Lord promises to regather His people, to restore and bless their land, and to judge the nations from Zion. Those who trust the Lord will be saved on Zion, but there, too, the Lord will pour out His wrath on those who have harmed His personal possession, Israel. Joel states the essential element of the eternal covenant between Israel and the Lord in the simple affirmation that Zion itself is His home.

Obadiah

7

INTRODUCTION TO OBADIAH

Obadiah, the shortest book in the Old Testament, is also one of the least understood. Many modern readers have a hard time comprehending its message; it seems strange and foreign. Obadiah appears to be very angry, even bitter, against Edom, but Edom is of little concern to us. We do not have the same reaction to the name that Judeans in Old Testament times had.

Yet it is important to study this brief prophetic book, if for no other reason than that it is part of the canon of Scripture. This alone means it is profitable for instruction in righteousness (2 Tim. 3:16), but most readers may find it more difficult to find such instruction from Obadiah than from other biblical books. Our hope is that this commentary will establish a basis for arriving at valid spiritual insights into the lasting and universal truths of the book of Obadiah.

The Prophet and His Times

Nothing much is known about Obadiah; his name means "servant of the Lord [Yahweh]." There is speculation that he was Ahab's steward (1 Kings 18:3–15) or King Jehoshaphat's official (2 Chron. 17:7), but these traditions are historically improbable.[1]

Most of the prophets have enough clues in the heading (the first verse) to determine at least an approximate date. Such is not the case with Obadiah; only a few hints within the main part of the book itself help to pinpoint a time when Obadiah lived. Three sorts of evidence have been presented for the date of Obadiah: historical allusions, its position within the twelve Minor Prophets, and literary connections with other prophets. The most objective kind of evidence would be a historical event mentioned in the book. Therefore, the references to history in Obadiah 10–14 will be discussed first.

HISTORICAL ALLUSIONS

A preliminary question is whether verses 12–14 were past or future to Obadiah at the time that he wrote them. It is not immediately clear from the English translations which is the correct decision. The translators of the KJV (see also the NRSV) took the verses as past tense: "But thou shouldest not have looked on the day of thy brother . . . ." Most modern versions, however, translate with a command or a warning. The NASB has, "Do not gloat over your brother's day," while the NIV has, "You should not look down on your brother in the day of his misfortune." If Obadiah's words are in fact meant as a command not to do something to the Edomites, then they should be taken as prior to any event to which they may refer.[2] It is more likely, however, that they are meant to have a rhetorical effect. In other words, the prophet portrays the past event of Edom's transgressions against Jerusalem more vividly by placing himself at the scene and demanding, as it were, that the Edomites cease their wicked behavior.[3]

The validity of this interpretation is confirmed by verses 10–11, which clearly depict a past event in which Edom became guilty and by the overall context of the book. Obadiah soundly condemns Edom for what it has done already, not for something it will do in the future. Finally, verse 15 refers only to the past behavior of the Edomites: "As you have done, it will be done to you." A similar literary device also occurs with reference to Edom in Lamentations 4:21: "Rejoice and be glad, O Daughter of Edom. . . . . But to you also the cup [of judgment] will be passed." There Jeremiah uses a sarcastic tone to "command" the Edomites to rejoice over Jerusalem's fall, even though interpreters unanimously agree that Jerusalem has already fallen.

In highly picturesque language, then, Obadiah focuses on the actions of Edom at a time of great catastrophe for Jerusalem. The word "day" occurs ten times in verses 10–14 (see NASB) of the disaster that befell the city, and it contrasts with "the day of the Lord" in verse 15, at which time the tables will be turned for Edom. During this period the Edomites sat by and gloated while foreigners entered Jerusalem, looted it, and took captives. Some of the Edomites also participated in the looting (perhaps after the departure of the foreigners) and prevented some of the city's inhabitants from fleeing. The Edomites, Judah's former allies, then either slaughtered the terrified refugees or captured them and turned them over to the enemy. The time is remembered as a period of "misfortune," "destruction," "trouble," "disaster," and "calamity."

In searching the history of Judah for a similar great catastrophe, the fall of the city to the Babylonians under Nebuchadnezzar in 586 B.C. immediately presents itself. At this time the Edomites should have been allies of Judah (Jer. 27:1–11); instead they encouraged the Babylonians (Ps. 137:7; see also Ezek. 25:12; 35:5–7). Moreover, despite the hostility of the Edomites some survivors did manage to make it to Edom (Jer. 40:11), possibly before the actual fall of Jerusalem.

It is true, as Leon Wood notes, that Obadiah does not describe the complete destruction of the city brought about by the Babylonians.[4] However, Obadiah focuses more on the guilt of Edom than on the event itself. For that matter Ezekiel, who clearly refers to the events of 586 B.C., gives even less detail about the destruction in his prophecy against Edom (25:12–15). One could wish Obadiah had been more explicit, but it was not necessary when his contemporaries remembered the details clearly.

The only other major contender for the historical incident underlying Obadiah 10–14 took place during the reign of Jehoram (848–841 B.C.).[5] This king of Judah tried unsuccessfully to put down an Edomite revolt against Judean control (2 Kings 8:20–21; 2 Chron. 21:8–10). Later the Philistines and Arabs invaded Judah (2 Chron. 21:16–17). About this attack we know very few details. The text says that the foreigners invaded Judah and "carried off all the goods found in the king's palace, together with his sons and wives. Not a son was left to [Jehoram] except Ahaziah, the youngest." From the term "king's palace" we can infer that Jerusalem was involved, but the extent to which the kind of general looting about which Obadiah speaks took place is unclear. Despite this raid, Jehoram continued as king in Jerusalem and the nation of Judah remained independent. The author of Kings did not even bother to include an account of it. Furthermore, the text of Chronicles remains silent about an Edomite role in this campaign. Amos speaks of Edom's pursuit of his brother with the sword (1:11), but his description is too general to be of any help.

In conclusion, the historical evidence points to the Babylonian destruction of Jerusalem in 586 B.C. as the background for Obadiah 10–14. Since Obadiah describes this event so vividly, it seems likely that he wrote the book not long after. Also, since Obadiah predicts the fall of Edom, he must have lived before that event. Most scholars think Edom fell near the end of the sixth century B.C. (see Mal. 1:2–5),[6] so Obadiah could not have written his book any later than that.

Canonical Position

Some interpreters think that Obadiah's position among the twelve Minor Prophets is important for its date. For example, Leon Wood says: "[Obadiah] falls among the first six of these prophets, all of which date to either the ninth or eighth centuries, while those that follow come from the seventh century, the exile, and finally after the exile. This placement would be strange if Obadiah were written as late as the time of the exile."[7]

The issue of chronology as a basis for ordering the Minor Prophets has been treated in the introduction to Joel, which the reader may consult for more details. Here let it be noted that Wood assumes that chronology was a major factor in the arrangement of the twelve Minor Prophets. Yet even among the first six books, the arrangement is not completely chronological, and the date of a third of those six (Joel and Obadiah) can by no means be established as preexilic.

LITERARY RELATIONS

Obadiah 1–9 and Jeremiah 49:7–16 have some remarkable similarities in expression and thought. Many have argued that close analysis shows that Jeremiah adapted the material from Obadiah and not the other way around.[8] If this were the case, Obadiah 1–9 could not be dated to after the fall of Jerusalem in 586 B.C.

Several factors must be considered before using these comparisons to place Obadiah relative to Jeremiah. First, it is notoriously difficult to determine in such situations who is quoting whom. Some expressions appear to be more original to Obadiah, but others seem to favor Jeremiah as the earlier source (e.g., "the terror you inspire," Jer. 49:16, is omitted by Obadiah, giving a smoother reading).

Second, various expressions the prophets used tended to become part of traditional language. Compare, for example, the discussion above about Joel and the other prophets who describe the "day of the Lord" in almost stereotyped phrases.

Third, the description of Edom's pride possibly derives from real boasts made by the Edomites themselves. Thus, the prophets could have known of sayings current among them, such as "We live in the clefts of the rocks," or "We have made our nest as high as an eagle's."

Fourth, given that some prophets who ministered in Israel did not record their sermons in book form (e.g., Elijah and Elisha), it is possible that Obadiah and Jeremiah could have both relied on earlier traditional language, reshaping their own unique prophecies under the inspiration of the Spirit of God.

Finally, one should not overstate the extent of the similarities between Obadiah and Jeremiah. They both have unique oracles with different points of emphasis.[9]

Conclusion about the Date of Obadiah

The relationship between Jeremiah and Obadiah is the major positive argument in favor of an early date for Obadiah, but it is not strong enough to overturn the historical and contextual evidence for placing the book after the fall of Jerusalem. Still, since explicit indications of the date are lacking, one should not be dogmatic.[10] Because it predicts the fall of Edom, 500 B.C. would be the latest possible time for the book to have been written.

Relations Between Edom and Israel

From the biblical point of view, the history of the struggles between Edom and Israel began when Jacob and Esau stirred within Rebekah's womb. She was so puzzled by the intensity of it that she asked the Lord about it, and He replied:

> Two nations are in your womb,
> and two peoples from within you will be separated;
> one people will be stronger than the other,
> and the older will serve the younger. (Genesis 25:23)

The prophecy began to be fulfilled when Esau came out first, with Jacob, the "heel-grabber," clinging to his brother's heel.

Soon we learn that Esau is also Edom (red), because he sold his birthright for the red lentil stew (Gen. 25:27–34). Jacob's name becomes Israel after his encounter with the mysterious figure at the Jabbok River near Peniel (Gen. 32:22–32). Thus, the prophetic blessing that Isaac bestows on his two sons highlights the great significance of the relationship between Israel and Edom.

Through a ruse Jacob deceives his father into giving him the blessing that rightfully belongs to Esau. The blessing calls for the Lord's favor, for fertility, and for mastery over his brother and his descendants (Gen. 27:27–29). Later, Esau arrives and both father and son realize the gravity of the situation. In response to Esau's strong weeping Isaac can only speak of a lack of fertility, a life of violent bloodshed, and service to his brother. Isaac does hold out one thread of hope, however: "But when you grow restless, you will throw his yoke from off your neck" (Gen. 27:40). In light of subsequent history, it might be best to see the latter statement as general rather than specific. On many different occasions Edom rebelled against his servile condition and succeeded in breaking the yoke.

After the two brothers pass off the scene, the nations undergo their separate developments. The next time they come into contact Edom is strong enough to refuse passage to the Israelites, who ask simply to journey by the king's highway, promising not to "turn to the right or to the left until we have passed through your territory" (Num. 20:17).

Not until the period of the early monarchy does Edom come under Israelite control. Saul fought against Edom (1 Sam. 14:47), and Doeg the Edomite was his servant, acting as an informant against David (1 Sam. 21:7; 22:9, 18; see also Psalm 52). David, in turn, made the Edomites his vassals and placed garrisons in their land (2 Sam. 8:14).

Solomon went so far as to build a fleet of ships in Ezion Geber in the land of Edom (1 Kings 9:26). Yet before the end of his reign the Lord had raised up Hadad the Edomite as his adversary (1 Kings 11:14–22).[11]

Some sixty or more years later we hear of Jehoshaphat of Judah (872–848 B.C.) and his control of Edom. When Moab and Ammon rebelled against Jehoshaphat, the Edomites apparently had a minor role in it (2 Chron. 20:10). On another occasion, when Jehoshaphat fought against Moab, the king of Edom accompanied him and Jehoram of Israel (2 Kings 3:9). Actually, the text informs us that the "king" of Edom was in reality only a "deputy" (1 Kings 22:47). Perhaps this reflects the direct control Jehoshaphat exercised; he himself appointed a deputy to govern Edom.

A more serious rebellion occurred during the reign of Jehoram of Judah (848–841 B.C.; also known as Joram), Jehoshaphat's son (2 Kings 8:20–22). At this time the Edomites established an independent monarchy, which lasted right up to the time of the narrator of the passage in Kings. Amaziah, the grandson of Jehoram, took Sela and renamed it Joktheel, slaying 10,000 Edomites in the process (2 Kings 14:7).[12] Edom seems to have remained independent (see Amos 1:11).[13]

During the last days of the southern kingdom, Edom joined with Judah and other allies, and they rebelled against Nebuchadnezzar of Babylon (Jer. 27:1–11). Yet when Nebuchadnezzar appeared in Palestine and overran Judah, the allies deserted. For this Edom comes in for severe condemnation in the Old Testament. Psalm 137:7 depicts the Edomites as cheering on the Babylonians with "Tear it down . . . tear it down to its foundations!" Lamentations is equally vivid in its rebuke:

> Rejoice and be glad, O daughter of Edom,
>   you who live in the land of Uz.
> But to you also the cup will be passed;
>   you will be drunk and stripped naked.
>   (Lamentations 4:21)

Ezekiel also denounces the Edomites for taking advantage of this opportunity to get revenge against their brother Judah (25:12; 35:5).

Edomite behavior on this occasion, then, forms the backdrop to Obadiah's condemnations (vv. 10–14). As a result of Edom's treachery, the people were able to occupy parts of southern Judah, especially in and around Hebron and the Negev.[14]

Late in the sixth or early in the fifth century B.C. certain Arab groups displaced the Edomites from their homeland. Obadiah apparently prophesied about this in verses 7–9. Many Edomites did stay in southern Judah, however, mixing with the Arabs. Later, this mixed population became known as Idumeans, and southern Judah was called Idumea. In the Maccabean and Hasmonean periods the Jews overwhelmed the Idumeans in this area. However, they were not able to drive them out completely, and a very astute Idumean, Herod the Great, eventually managed to become king of all Judea.[15]

The Message of Obadiah for Today

Many modern readers of Obadiah might agree with J. Alberto Soggin, who says that Obadiah's book is of little theological interest.[16] If one focuses on the apparently narrow perspective of a people's outrage against an ally that betrayed them and of their longing for revenge, one might possibly concur. However, the themes of the book have a much broader theological interest.

Edom, first of all, stands as a type of all those who oppose the purposes of the Lord.[17] This is made plain when the perspective shifts, at verses 15–21, from Edom alone to Edom and all the nations. Other places in Scripture that describe the Lord's coming to earth for judgment also depict Edom in similar terms (Judg. 5:4; Isa. 63:1–6; see comments on Obad. 1a–b below). Edom's treachery against a sister nation and its unbounded confidence in its own invulnerability made it a perfect example for the theological truths taught in the book. Whatever Obadiah says about Edom applies equally to any nation that sets itself against the Lord and His people.

The book of Obadiah also has much to say about the kingdom of God. The closing statement proclaims, "And the kingdom will be the Lord's." The truth of this credo becomes increasingly plain throughout the book as we see that the Lord is sovereign over the nations. He issues the summons for the nations to assemble against Edom (v. 1b); He challenges Edom's proud security (vv. 2–4); He threatens to cut off all hope of rescue (vv. 8–9); and He promises a day for righting all wrongs, restoring Israel and Judah to their former territories (vv. 15–21).

Obadiah, in common with other prophets, sees the messianic kingdom established on the earth, with Mount Zion as the center of authority. The people of Israel, whether of the southern or northern tribes, will return to the land and join together to win back their territory with the Lord's aid. They will then rule over the rest of the nations.

Structure and Outline of Obadiah

Like the prophecy of Joel, that of Obadiah deals with both

history and the eschatological Day of the Lord. Both prophets also predict judgment on the nations and a great deliverance for Judah. Yet Obadiah dwells on the fortunes of only one nation—Edom.

The fate of the Edomites is presented in two parts, separated by a description of their cruel treatment of Jerusalem. According to the first part (vv. 1b–9), the Lord will stir up the nations to conquer Edom. Since the center section of Obadiah (vv. 10–14) shows how the Edomites turned against Judah, their ally, it is fitting that the nations who subdue Edom will include her own friends. Just as Edomites stood at the crossroads and cut down the refugees from Jerusalem, so others will cut off all the Edomites from the territory of Esau in this first phase of the judgment.

A second outpouring of wrath awaits Edom in the great Day of the Lord. Then Edom will share the sentence of all the nations, but Obadiah stresses the role of the Lord's people, Israel, who will avenge themselves of the wicked nations' role in Judah's great catastrophe. This time Israel will be saved and possess the territories of her former enemies.

I. The Nations Invade Edom (1–9)
  A. Heading (1a–b)
  B. The Lord Summons the Nations for Battle (1c–d)
  C. The Lord Pulls Down Edom's Defenses (2–4)
  D. The Allies Plunder Edom's Treasures (5–7)
  E. The Lord Destroys Edom's Resources (8–9)
II. Edom Betrays Judah (10–14)
  A. Edom Acts Violently Against His Brother Jacob (10)
  B. Edom Contributes to Jerusalem's Trouble (11–14)
III. The Lord Judges Edom in the Day of the Lord (15–21)
  A. The Lord Judges the Nations for How They Treated Israel (15–16)
  B. Israel Possesses Edom and the Nations (17–21)

8

THE NATIONS INVADE EDOM

Obadiah 1–9

In the first part of his book, Obadiah blends the Lord's judgment of Edom with the way the nations actually carry it out. The Lord summons armies to attack the Edomites as His instrument of judgment. Edom smugly thinks itself completely secure because it is located in a mountainous region that is easily defended, but the Lord will bring down the proud nation and open it up to marauders, using treachery by Edom's own allies. They will set an ambush, and the Edomites will fall into it unaware. In this way the Lord will bring to nothing all the wise counsel of the nation's strategists and remove the Edomites completely from their territory.

Heading (1a–b)

The general heading to Obadiah identifies the book as the "vision of Obadiah." This refers specifically to a prophetic vision or revelation from the Lord. A second heading also occurs: "This is what the Sovereign Lord says to Edom." Many of the modern versions, including the NIV, translate "about Edom" instead of "to Edom." The original could imply either that Edom is the general subject of the vision or that the Lord speaks directly to the nation in the vision. The latter interpretation seems to be confirmed when we observe that throughout the book the Lord also addresses Himself directly to Edom.[18]

Why should this be? In its original setting Obadiah would have delivered his message directly to the Judeans, who had recently watched their city burn to the ground with looters ransacking it while the Edomites cheered on the enemy. By addressing Edom so directly, Obadiah creates a strong emotional response in his audience. It is as though the Edomites stand before the people while the Lord, through His prophet, soundly condemns them. Ultimately, the deeds and fate of Jacob's brother serve as an example as well as an encouragement for his descendants. In a broader sense, this small book warns those nations and individuals who do not serve the Lord, and it has a lesson for those who do follow Him.

The Lord Summons the Nations for Battle (1c–d)

Obadiah sees a vision of a messenger who will go out with word that the nations should prepare for battle against Edom. All is well, for the message originates with the Lord Himself. He controls the counsels for this war, though the nations may make plans among themselves without realizing the true source of those plans. The language is a dramatic way of stating the theological truth that the Lord will stir up the nations to do battle against Edom. Of course, there will be some political pretext, but the Lord stands behind all human plans.

As the prophecy unfolds, it becomes clear that this council of war is future to Obadiah. He views the war council in his vision and reports on it as though it has already happened ("we have heard"). However, at the end of verse 7 ("those who eat your bread will set a trap for you") and then in verses 8–9, he returns to normal language for presenting future events.

After the Lord has initiated the action, a messenger goes out to alert the allies of the moment for action. The original Hebrew text uses repetition to stress the urgency of the envoy's words: "Rise up! Come on, let's rise up against her for battle!" The confident expectation of victory then contrasts vividly with the picture of Edom's sense of security in the verses that follow.

THE LORD PULLS DOWN EDOM'S DEFENSES (2–4)

Edom was located south of the Dead Sea, being bounded on the north by the Wadi Zered. The other borders are uncertain, but the country included much of the rugged terrain between the deep depression of the Arabah on the west, the desert on the east, and the Gulf of Aqaba on the south.

The blessings of geography made the Edomites confident that they could maintain their independence, but the Lord declares that the highest place imaginable cannot save the proud nation from judgment. Wherever they are, the Lord will bring them down and open them up to foreign armies.

According to verse 2, Edom may think that it is important and secure, but the Lord has actually given it a reduced position among the world powers.[19] It is not a superpower like Babylon or Assyria. Later the Lord promises to reduce it to nothing (vv. 9, 18).

A deep undercurrent of divine sovereignty flows through verse 3. A nation only deceives itself if it hopes to ensure its own safety through human effort. Nothing can stop God's arm from reaching anywhere to pull down arrogant strongholds. The verse closes with a concrete illustration of Edom's self-deception: "Who can bring me down to the ground?" The reader knows the answer: the Lord can do it.

Edom lives "in the clefts of the rocks" (v. 3), and the term for "rocks" is also the name of the capital city, Sela. Previously this had been identified with modern Petra (which also means "rock" in Greek), but more recent archaeological research places it farther to the north at the modern village of Sela, about two and a half miles northwest of Bozrah.[20]

The Edomite boast of verse 4 seems absurd next to the power of the Lord. No eagle can fly high enough to escape His hand. If a people were capable of building even among the stars, could they elude there the God whose own dwelling place is in heaven (see Amos 9:2–4)?

The Allies Plunder Edom's Treasures (5–7)

Once the Lord has pulled down the Edomites from the heights, their great wealth will be opened up to foreign invaders. Edom's own trusted allies ("your allies," "your friends," "those who eat your bread," v. 7) will set an ambush and rout its army. The Lord, who uses the nations to accomplish His purpose, judges Edom thoroughly. Thieves and grape gatherers would not devastate the nation so completely as the Lord. *They* would leave something behind, but nothing will remain after the Lord brings Edom down from the lofty heights.

Obadiah, suddenly struck by the horror of Edom's plight, interrupts the discussion about thieves and robbers with an astonished exclamation (v. 5). To paraphrase, "If mere thieves came to you—but oh, how much worse it will be for you when the Lord Himself sends judgment!"

Since so little is known about Edomite history, it is difficult to determine the precise incident referred to in verse 7. Assuming that Obadiah writes soon after the fall of Jerusalem in 586 B.C., he could be predicting how the Arabs would displace the Edomites from their homeland, a conflict that occurred near the end of the sixth century B.C.[21] The allies might be the Persians or even the Arabs themselves. "But you will not detect it" is literally "there is no understanding in it." The Edomites will fall into the trap completely unawares. The line makes a nice transition to verse 8. Edom, which was noted for wisdom (compare Eliphaz the Temanite in Job 2:11; Jer. 49:7), will lose all sense and be deceived by her enemies.

The Lord Destroys Edom's Resources (8–9)

Obadiah interweaves nicely the themes of divine intervention and human instrumentality. He began with a council of war by the nations, but the message to commence the battle came from the Lord Himself. Then the Lord's personal role in pulling Edom down from its lofty position came into focus, followed by an ambush set by Edom's allies that made it possible to plunder her. At the end of the passage the prophet returns to the theme of the Lord as the one who originates the judgment. Will the Edomites fall into the trap unawares? That is only because the Lord will destroy wise counsel from the nation. The army will look for capable guidance in a crisis but find none. As a result, the invaders will slaughter the population completely.

"That day" (v. 8) often refers in the prophets to the Day of the Lord at the end of the age. Here it continues the prophecy of the attack by other nations, but it also highlights the Lord's personal role in the judgment. It will have the quality of a day of the Lord against Edom, though she will also be present for that final judgment along with all the nations (v. 15).

Teman (v. 9) may refer to a region rather than a city, possibly to the southern part of Edom. In verse 9 it stands for the whole nation (as in Jer. 49:20). When battle strategies fail, the warriors panic. Some of the Edomites would be expelled across the borders; the rest were to die in fierce fighting. The enemy would completely empty the country of its original inhabitants. It is evidently from the offspring of those who were exiled that a new coalition of Edomites will arise against Israel and be judged in the great day of the Lord (v. 15; see Joel 3:19).

In Hebrew the expression "all" or "every" often means a majority or a very large number. For example, David struck down "all the men in Edom" (1 Kings 11:15), yet the nation of Edom continued. Also Amos, uniquely among the prophets, speaks of a "remnant" for Edom that will continue into the millennial kingdom (9:12). Even this remnant will be Israel's possession, but it must consist of individual Edomites who will profess the name of the Lord (see Joel 2:32). Exactly how God will raise up the descendants of Edom for a renewed battle against Israel in the end times remains a mystery. Yet He surely is capable of accomplishing it, just as He will bring all of the Jewish people back to their land.

9

EDOM BETRAYS JUDAH

OBADIAH 10–14

A long history of bitter relations between Judah and Edom culminated with Edom's role in the Babylonian capture and destruction of Jerusalem in 586 B.C. (see "Introduction: Obadiah"). Edom should have fought alongside the Judeans; instead they stood aloof, helped themselves to the spoils, and actively prevented refugees from escaping. The Jews became especially bitter because they believed they had been betrayed. The Lord assured His people that justice would be done. Edom, according to Obadiah 7–8, will itself become the victim of treachery.

EDOM ACTS VIOLENTLY AGAINST HIS BROTHER JACOB (10)

Obadiah takes a family perspective on the relationship between Judah and Edom. The two nations began as the twin brothers Jacob and Esau. Yet "violence" summarizes the long history of relations between these two peoples. On many occasions Edom acted cruelly toward his brother, but the culminating act of violence was in his betrayal of Judah at a time when the two countries were allies. Because of this violence Edom will be cut off as a nation.

A close connection exists for the cultures of the Old Testament period between a nation's "shame" and its destruction. Thus, Joel urged the priests to entreat the Lord not to make His "inheritance an object of scorn, a byword among the nations" (Joel 2:17). Later, the Lord responded: "Never again will my people be shamed" (Joel 2:27). For Obadiah there is a contrast with Edom's haughty pride (v. 3). The once-proud people will be put to shame because they will have lost everything.

Edom Contributes to Jerusalem's Trouble (11–14)

Edom's behavior became progressively worse at the time of Jerusalem's downfall. First, they simply stood by and watched while the Babylonian forces took the city. In this they also became guilty, since as allies they should have come to their brother's aid (see Jer. 27:1–11). They could have stayed their distance and watched in horror, but instead they also rejoiced and boasted about what was happening to the people of Jerusalem. Next they actually entered the city to take whatever share of the loot they could. At the same time they made sure none escaped, handing over all survivors to the Babylonians. This was the behavior that finally filled up their guilt and brought on the stinging denunciations of Obadiah, Jeremiah, Ezekiel, and Joel.

Obadiah's message is reinforced by the structure of the passage itself. In verses 10–11 Obadiah recounts for the Edomites what they have done, indicating their doom at the same time. Then in verses 12–14 he admonishes the Edomites, telling them what they should not do. Verses 12–14 also have a structure that highlights a sequence that moves from outside (v. 12) to inside (v. 13) and then back outside the city (v. 14). The prophet focuses our attention on the scene (entering and surveying the shameful destruction that has taken place) by a reversed structure. In the middle section, when he moves inside the city, Obadiah repeats or parallels many of the previous phrases, something not always obvious from the English:

- "entered his gates" (v. 11) = "march through [lit., 'enter'] the gates of my people" (v. 13)

- "his wealth" (v. 11) = "their wealth" (v. 13)
- "the day of his misfortune" (v. 12) = "the day of their disaster" (v. 13)
- "the day of their trouble" (v. 12) = "the day of their trouble" (v. 14)
- "look down on" (v. 12) = "look down on" (v. 13).

Obadiah slows down the action that takes place in the city itself by repeating these expressions.

According to various biblical passages, the Edomites did not enter the city directly with the Babylonians (Ps. 137:7; Lam. 4:21; Ezek. 25:12–14; Joel 3:19). Rather, they watched nearby and waited for their opportunity (Obad. 11), much like vultures waiting to feed on a carcass after the lions are finished. One of the apocryphal books (1 Esd. 4:45) has the Edomites actually burning the temple, but this is evidently due to later reflection on and amplification of the biblical statements.

As discussed in the introduction, it is best to take the various instances of "you should not" in verses 12–14 as rhetorical. The prophet places himself alongside the Edomites, as it were, and tries to stop them from doing what they did.

Obadiah uses five terms in verses 12–14 to describe the "day" of disaster that befell Judah. The first one, "his misfortune," occurs elsewhere only in Job 31:3 ("disaster" in the NIV), where it parallels "ruin," the same word translated "disaster" in Obadiah (three times in v. 13). When the prophet refers to "the day of his misfortune," he singles out a specific period of time when great calamity came upon Judah and Jerusalem. The second term, "their destruction," is quite strong and makes it unlikely that Obadiah means an event prior to the destruction of Jerusalem by the Babylonians in 586 B.C. The third term, "their trouble," occurs at the end of verse 12 and again at the end of verse 14. It is used in Jeremiah 30:7 of the "time of trouble for Jacob" that forms part of the eschatological day of the Lord (see Zeph. 1:15).[22] Several times in Jeremiah the word refers to the anguish that accompanies a painful childbirth (Jer. 4:31; 6:24; 49:24; 50:43). The fourth term, "disaster," is repeated three times in verse 13. The fifth of Obadiah's terms is "calamity," the only one that is not directly connected with "day." The dual expression, "in their calamity in the day of their disaster," underlines the shameful guilt of the Edomites: they are gloating even while they survey the ruins of the city.

Obadiah forbids the Edomites to "boast" over Judah's misfortune (v. 12). The Hebrew is quite expressive: "And do not make great with your mouth" (see Ezek. 35:13). Allen translates, "Do not talk so big." He also suggests a close relationship between the boasting here and that of verse 3.[23] The boasting would include belittling and taunting Judah so as to make the braggarts seem superior. The Edomites felt that what happened to Judah could never happen to them.

At verse 14 the scene shifts again to outside Jerusalem. Refugees are fleeing the Babylonian army, but the Edomites stand in their way and cruelly cut them down. The action could have been simultaneous with the looting depicted in verse 13 if it was done by additional Edomites who did not enter the city. More likely, however, it happened while the Edomites stood at a safe distance and gloated. The arrangement of the verses is not chronological, but for its rhetorical effect of making the inside of Jerusalem the center of the stage. Just as Edom "cut down" Judean fugitives, so shall Edomites be "cut off" by slaughter when the Lord judges them (Obad. 9).

10

THE LORD JUDGES EDOM IN THE DAY OF THE LORD

OBADIAH 15–21

Edom's judgment is twofold. First, the nation will suffer at the hands of other nations (vv. 1b–9). Later, however, it will suffer at the hands of the Lord and at the hands of His people. It is this later judgment that verses 15–21 emphasize.

Verses 15–16 refer in a general way to the judgment against Edom and the nations, based on the way they have dealt with Israel. That is, they will be judged in the same measure and in the same manner as they have mistreated Israel. Next, verses 17–21 talk about the salvation of Israel and their return from captivity. Consequently, the Israelites will take possession of the same lands from which Edom and the nations exiled them.

The Lord is active throughout this period. It is His "day" when He brings to an end the era when the nations control the world. He pours out His wrath, rescues and restores His people, and finally establishes His kingdom on earth.

THE LORD JUDGES THE NATIONS FOR HOW THEY TREATED ISRAEL (15–16)

The first (v. 8) and last (v. 15) occurrences of "day" in Obadiah refer to the time when the Lord acts against the enemies of

His people. All the references in between are to the "day" of distress and anguish experienced by Judah and Jerusalem. Edom alone stood under the Lord's judgment the first time; now all the nations, including Edom, will have to suffer the full force of the Lord's fury.

If Judah, the Lord's people, had a "day of distress" at the hands of the Edomites and Babylonians, an even greater "day" looms on the horizon, according to verse 15. This day belongs to the Lord, and He will pour out His wrath on all the nations of the earth (see Joel 1:15; 2:1, 31; Amos 5:18–20). Edom cannot expect to escape this judgment, and the prophet's announcement brings to a halt the sounds of merriment and boasting.

The justice of God demands that unrighteousness in a nation be punished. As is so often the case in the prophets, Obadiah here announces that the punishment will fit the crime. The Edomites betrayed Judah; the nations will betray Edom (v. 7). The Edomites killed or betrayed the refugees; the Lord will cut off all Edomites from their land (v. 9). They boasted against Judah; their shame will last forever (v. 10). Edom dealt violently with his brother; Jacob and Joseph will be like fire burning among the Edomite chaff (v. 18). Edom took the possessions of his brother; the whole nation of Israel will dispossess Edom (vv. 19–20).

The Lord uses an interesting figurative expression when He says that Edom and the nations will "drink continually" (v. 16). One might expect looters to become drunk with wine, but the expression means that Jerusalem herself is like a cup filled with a drink that will intoxicate all the nations (see Isa. 51:22; Zech. 12:2). God's wrath is often described as "wine" in Scripture (Pss. 60:3; 75:8; Jer. 25:15; 51:7; Rev. 14:10; 16:19; 19:15). Evidently the nations become drunk with God's wrath when they attack Jerusalem or His people. More precisely, the attack makes them deserving of wrath just as surely as wine makes its abusers stagger and fall.

Edom's judgment will correspond to its deed. The people made a mockery of God's holy hill by their drunken actions against defenseless Judah. In so doing they became drunk with the wrath of God. The wrath was not expressed immediately, but the Edomites are still filled with it. In the future all the nations will imbibe heavily of this wrath. They will even drink more as they again attack Jerusalem and Judah, until at last the wine itself will destroy them.

Some argue that the Lord addresses Judah, not Edom in verse 15.[24] In this case it means that just as Judah suffered the wrath of the nations, so the nations will suffer God's wrath. It is true that the Hebrew word for "you" is singular in verse 15 and plural in verse 16, but for cases where a nation is viewed as an individual, such alternation between singular and plural is not unusual.[25] In any case, it is very difficult to accept that Judah is suddenly introduced with only a pronoun. The ancient versions continue to make Edom the center of attention.

At first glance Obadiah appears to say that no trace of the nations will remain, yet there will be a remnant of various nations in the Millennium (Isa. 2:2–4; Amos 9:12; Mic. 4:1–3; Zech. 14:16–19). How are these two ideas to be reconciled? The answer perhaps lies in the difference between the concept of nations before and during the Millennium. Before the golden age of Messiah's rule on earth, the nations consider themselves sovereign and fight to maintain their individual rights. When Christ returns, however, only those from the nations who have called on the Lord's name will enter. Also, they will be under one King and no longer a threat to Israel's existence. Therefore, the nations as we presently know them will exist no more once the Millennium begins. In any case, Obadiah dwells only on the destruction of the old order as far as the nations are concerned.

Israel Possesses Edom and the Nations (17–21)

The day of the Lord will dawn with judgment for the nations, but salvation for Israel. At the end of his book, Obadiah turns to the changing fortunes of God's chosen people in that day. The two parts of the nation will reunite and possess their former territories, expanding into what was formerly Edomite land. Thus, the situation in Obadiah's own day, when Judah and Israel were scattered and Jerusalem was humbled, will completely reverse itself.

At the fall of Jerusalem in 586 B.C. the survivors were cruelly killed or delivered to the enemy. When the Lord returns, however, there will be survivors (v. 17). He will see to it that all who call upon His name will escape (see comments on Joel 2:32; also Zech. 14:1–5).

The "house of Jacob" stands for all Israel, north and south (v. 18), but it also emphasizes Edom as the brother of Jacob (v. 10). In its present form the text means that Israel will regain its former land, which was its "inheritance" (v. 17; see Ex. 6:8; Ezek. 11:15).

Some passages, like verse 18, speak of a military participation by Israel in the judgment of the nations just prior to the Millennium (Zech. 12:1–9; Mal. 4:3), while others depict the Lord carrying out the judgment on behalf of His people (Joel 3:12; Zech. 14:3–5; cf. Matt. 25:31–46). It is difficult to reconstruct the precise order of events. In any case, much of the material is not strictly chronological, but that is not unusual for prophecies of the distant future. Zechariah 12–14, for example, opens with the events surrounding the establishment of the millennial kingdom (12:1–13:6), suddenly switches back to the rejection of Christ at the first Advent (13:7), continues with the separation of a righteous remnant of Jews through their trials among the nations (13:8–10), and finally returns to the events that usher in the Millennium (chap. 14).

Tentatively, it would seem that when the nations come against Jerusalem they are at first victorious (Zech. 14:2). Then the Lord gives His people divine strength in battle, and shortly after that He pours out His Spirit on them (Joel 2:28; Zech. 12:10) and Christ returns in the company of angelic hosts (or possibly saints; Zech. 14:3–5). It is not impossible that the Spirit is poured out more than once during the Tribulation period, even as it was poured out more than once during the foundational era of the church (Acts 2; 10:44–48). In any event, when Christ returns He will determine those nations or individuals to be included in or excluded from the millennial kingdom.

The name "Jacob" would include the entire family of Israel, but the "house of Joseph" is added to make it clear that the Lord will reassemble the northern kingdom, which had been destroyed by the Assyrians, to inherit their former territory (cf. Amos 9:8–9). For the figure of Israel fighting its enemies like a flame among highly combustible material, see Zechariah 12:6.

For the problem of the "remnant of Edom" in Amos 9:12, see the comments on Obadiah 9. Armerding finds a preliminary historical fulfillment when Judas Maccabaeus defeated the Idumeans in 166 B.C. and afterward when John Hyrcanus brought them into submission by 125 B.C. Armerding goes on to state: The Idumeans "continued to haunt the Jews, however, for the family of Herod the Great was of Idumaean descent; but after the second century B.C., they had virtually been consumed by the house of Jacob, to which they lost their national identity and autonomy."[26]

Idumea is the name for the territory of Edom found in the Greek Old Testament (LXX) and Josephus. After the conquest of Judah, the Edomites began to occupy parts of southern Judah itself, especially in and around Hebron and the Negev. Various Arabian groups (eventually the Nabateans) took over the former territory of Edom, but some Edomites managed to maintain their identity in southern Judah.[27] Therefore, one could speak of a partial fulfillment of Obadiah's oracle when the Maccabeans and Hasmoneans reclaimed these areas for Israel.

Several factors should be kept in mind, however. First, Obadiah speaks of the final day of the Lord when all the nations will be judged before the Lord establishes the messianic kingdom. Second, a remnant from the exiles of the Ephraimites must play a large role in the fulfillment of the prophecy. Third, the term Idumea can be vague; not all Idumeans are necessarily "of the house of Esau." Finally, Armerding is correct to note that Herod and his descendants still plagued Israel even after the assimilation of the Idumeans.

Verses 19 and 20 list the Israelite territory possessed before the Exile, expanding on the statement that "the house of Jacob will possess its inheritance" (v. 17). Edom is the only new territory that becomes Israelite.[28]

The Negev in Old Testament times included only the northern part of the modern Negev.[29] As discussed in the introduction, Edom may have conquered much of Judean territory in the

Negev around the time the Babylonians destroyed Jerusalem.

The "foothills" (the Shephelah) are consist of low hills and broad valleys between the Philistine territory along the coastal plain and the Judean hill country. The Israelites will expand their borders from previous territory, but not beyond the boundaries the Lord set for them (Josh. 15:45–47).

From the original Hebrew of verse 19 it is difficult to determine who is to possess Ephraim and Samaria. Some of the versions, including the NIV, seem to imply that those of the Negev and foothills will possess these northern areas of Israel. Yet if "the house of Joseph" (v. 18) participates, it is hard to imagine why Judeans would take over their territory. The text probably means that exiles from Ephraim and Samaria will possess their former territories.

The last line of verse 19 turns to Benjamin. Saul, the first king of Israel and a Benjamite, won Jabesh Gilead for Israel from the Ammonites (1 Sam. 11:1–11). Later, Abner set up Ish-Bosheth, a son of Saul, as king over Gilead and Israel (2 Sam. 2:8–11). Perhaps this background helps explain the expansion of Benjamin into the territory across the Jordan which would otherwise have belonged to Manasseh.

From the standpoint of the Hebrew text, verse 20 is the most difficult in the entire book of Obadiah to interpret. The NIV is probably correct to indicate that the exiles living in Canaan will have a separate inheritance which will extend as far as Zarephath (see also the KJV). The passage emphasizes that Israel will extend her former territory in the coming kingdom.

Zarephath was a Phoenician coastal town roughly midway between Tyre and Sidon. It is best known as the site where Elijah lived at the house of a widow and her son until the Lord was about to give relief to Israel from a great drought (1 Kings 17:7–24).

Obadiah predicts that the former inhabitants of Jerusalem (and possibly also the Israelite exiles) will expand into the Negev, but verse 19 already mentioned Judeans in the Negev who will possess Edomite territory. Since the Edomites began to take over the area of the Negev shortly after the fall of Jerusalem, however, the text simply explains that the returned exiles will not only inhabit old territories, but also extend into those of their enemies. Also, there seems to be some distinction between the Negev in general and the "towns" of the Negev. Perhaps there is thought of Levites in Jerusalem taking possession of the towns of southern Judah (compare Josh. 21).

Sepharad is quite difficult to identify. Some ancient versions refer to it as Spain, but many modern interpreters prefer Sardis in Asia Minor.[30] That might force the interpreter to move the date of Obadiah into the Persian period, but the historical problems are too complex to exclude the possibility of an earlier Judean colony at Sardis.

Another interesting suggestion is Saparda, an area of ancient Media where Sargon II settled prisoners from Syria-Palestine.[31] One problem is that the phrase "exiles from Jerusalem" makes us think of the mass deportations by the Babylonians between 605 and 586 B.C. rather than a much earlier deportation by the Assyrian king Sargon II, for which there is no independent biblical evidence.

Who are the "deliverers" who "govern" from Mt. Zion the Edomites, according to verse 21? In the period between the conquest and the monarchy, the Lord would raise up a "deliverer" when the Israelites cried out because of foreign oppression (Judg. 3:9, 15). Some of these deliverers also acted as judges or leaders for the people of Israel. Nehemiah 9:27 refers to all the judges collectively as "deliverers." Evidently Obadiah intends to make some reference to this period of the Judges. Just as the Lord raised up the judges of old to rescue His people, so in the future similar leaders will arise to save Israel from the oppression of the nations. Here "the mountains of Esau" is intended as a type to include all the enemies of God's people.

In this way the verse calls to mind the promise that "on Mount Zion will be deliverance" (v. 17). Mount Zion is the place where the Lord will deliver His people and then enable them to conquer their enemies. Perhaps there is also the additional thought that these saviors will continue to exercise authority over the nations in the millennial kingdom.

When the time arrives for the Lord to judge the nations and deliver Israel, He will set up a kingdom that will endure forever (see Dan. 7:26–27). Obadiah seems strange to some because it draws out the theme of judgment on Edom. Yet Edom is only one of the nations that will feel the Lord's wrath. It stands out for its pride and violent treatment of the covenant people. In the overall picture, then, the struggles between Israel and Edom highlight a broader theme of good against evil, of the people of God against the people of Satan (compare Gen. 3:14–15). That struggle finally culminates in an earthly kingdom set up by Christ when He returns to rule all the nations from Jerusalem. In the New Testament the book of Revelation picks up these topics and develops them in terms of Babylon as the great representative of evil on earth (Rev. 17–18). Obadiah closes his prophecy with one of the strongest statements of the universal sovereignty of the Lord in the entire Bible: "And the kingdom will be the Lord's."

Micah

11

INTRODUCTION TO MICAH

THE PROPHET AND HIS TIMES

In contrast to Joel and Obadiah, it is easy to determine the date and historical background for the book of Micah. The first verse of the book (the "heading") sets the background; Micah's ministry occurred during the reigns of Jotham, Ahaz, and Hezekiah—kings of Judah. By comparing the biblical data in the books of Kings and Chronicles with historical data from Assyria, Babylonia, and Egypt, it is possible to establish the period of reign for these kings of Judah at about 750–690 B.C.[1] Also, since Micah predicts the fall of Samaria, the bulk of his ministry should probably be dated prior to 722 B.C. Finally, even though Micah lived at a time when both the northern kingdom of Israel and the southern kingdom of Judah had their own kings, he did not mention any of Israel's kings in the heading to his book. This may be because his ministry began after the death of Jeroboam II, during a period about which the Lord says through Hosea, "They [the kingdom of Israel] set up kings without my consent" (Hos. 8:4).[2] Thus, Micah must have ministered between about 750–725 B.C.

It is more important, though, to know the events that were shaping Micah's world during his ministry than its precise chronological limits. For this there is a wealth of information in the chapters of Kings and Chronicles that deal with the relevant kings of Judah and Israel.[3]

JUDAH UNDER JOTHAM (750–735 B.C.)

Jotham reigned in Jerusalem for sixteen years (2 Kings 15:32–33), taking over the kingdom when his father, Azariah (also known as Uzziah), could no longer rule because of his leprosy (2 Kings 15:5). Jotham was a righteous king, but he failed to remove the "high places," where "the people continued to offer sacrifices and burn incense" (2 Kings 15:35). These "high places" were a continual stumbling block to the people in their worship of the Lord, often leading to a mixing of worship of the Lord with worship of idols (1 Kings 14:23; 2 Kings 16:4; 17:9–13). No wonder that the author of Chronicles called what went on at the high places "corrupt practices" (2 Chron. 27:2). It seems unusual that many righteous kings in Judah prior to the time of Hezekiah (2 Kings 18:4) and Josiah (2 Kings 23:5) would not do away with such sinful ways. Perhaps there were political ramifications that they were afraid to deal with, or possibly they did not care to reform the popular religion of the people. Even some of the kings of Judah, though, were more directly involved, especially Ahaz (2 Kings 16:3–4) and Manasseh (2 Kings 21:2–3).

Jotham inherited a kingdom from his father that was militarily strong and that had expanded into some of the territory that had been lost in previous times (2 Chron. 26:6–15). He strengthened Judah by building towns and fortresses in the Judean hill country, and he also rebuilt the Upper Gate of the temple and the wall that was part of the old city of David (2 Chron. 27:3–4). There is reason to think that a party in Judah that favored positive relations with Assyria deposed Jotham and installed his son Ahaz over the kingdom a few years before Jotham actually died (see 2 Kings 15:30). Also, Ahaz may have already been coregent with Jotham since 742 B.C. (based on 2 Kings 17:1).[4]

Early in Micah's ministry, then, the kingdom of Judah was strong politically and militarily, but there were already signs of a serious need for religious reforms. That need became much more evident during the reign of Jotham's son Ahaz.

Judah under Ahaz (742–716 B.C.)

Ahaz corrupted the worship of the Lord in Judah by adopting the idolatrous practices of the northern kingdom of Israel, by replacing the bronze altar that Solomon had built with an altar based on an Aramean (Syrian) model, and by changing other parts of the temple in Jerusalem (2 Kings 16:2–4, 10–18). He also "sacrificed his son in the fire" (2 Kings 16:3),[5] a practice that was loathsome to the Lord and that Micah the prophet condemned (Mic. 6:7).

With regard to foreign policy, Ahaz sought Assyrian intervention when a coalition of Israel and Aram (Syria) attacked Judah. This meant that Judah became something of a vassal nation to the king of Assyria (2 Kings 16:5–9, 18). The Assyrian nation was responsible for the downfall of the nations of Israel and Aram, both of which were incorporated into the Assyrian empire.

Conditions in Judah deteriorated considerably during the reign of Ahaz, both religiously and politically. It seems reasonable to assume that Micah conducted the bulk of his ministry during the time of Ahaz's sole reign. According to a possible interpretation of the biblical data (2 Kings 18:1, 9, 14), Hezekiah, the son of Ahaz, was made coregent at the age of fifteen with his father, who continued to live and to exercise some measure of control of the country for another ten years.[6]

Judah under Hezekiah (728–697 B.C.)

It is surprising that a wicked king like Ahaz would have a son who would turn the nation back to serving the Lord. Perhaps the prophets Micah and Isaiah had some influence on the young prince even before he became sole ruler when his father died. Hezekiah, unlike his predecessors, tore down the high places and other symbols of idolatry (2 Kings 18:4). The author of Kings was very impressed: "There was no one like him among all the kings of Judah, either before him or after him. He held fast to the Lord and did not cease to follow him; he kept the commands the Lord had given Moses" (2 Kings 18:5–6).

The Chronicler was more detailed in his praise of Hezekiah and mentioned even a general Passover celebration that included all Israel, "from Beersheba to Dan" (2 Chron. 30:5). The prophet Isaiah focused on the contrast between Hezekiah and his father Ahaz. Isaiah had to seek out the father, who then refused to accept a sign from the Lord (Isa. 7:1–12). The son, however, immediately turned to the Lord in a crisis and also received a miraculous sign from the Lord that confirmed his healing (Isa. 37:1–20; 38:1–8).

Hezekiah's attitude toward the Assyrians was ambiguous to an extent. He seems to have submitted at first, paying tribute to King Sennacherib (2 Kings 18:13–16). Later the Lord delivered Jerusalem from Sennacherib, largely because of Hezekiah's prayers to the Lord (2 Kings 19:20; Isa. 37:14–37). An account of this great conflict in Israel's history is found among the Assyrian annals as well as in the Bible. Sennacherib boasts that he shut up Hezekiah in Jerusalem "like a bird in a cage,"[7] but he significantly omits any mention of capturing the city. Such an omission was tantamount to admitting that he suffered a defeat. The Bible describes the defeat: "the angel of the Lord went out and put to death a hundred and eighty-five thousand men in the Assyrian camp," and Sennacherib returned to Nineveh (2 Kings 19:35–36).

Judah and Jerusalem must have been focal points of activity in the time of Hezekiah. Hezekiah's representatives traveled throughout the country tearing down the worship places and destroying all remnants of idolatry. Word came that Sennacherib was approaching, and quickly the people tried to fortify the towns and especially Jerusalem. Hezekiah evidently constructed the famous tunnel that kept the water source within the city walls at this time (2 Kings 20:20). After the failure of the human efforts, including the attempt to buy off Sennacherib, Hezekiah set the example for the people in turning to the Lord for help. Unfortunately, as the prophets Micah and Isaiah were able to discern, the reformation of the country did not reach very deeply into the hearts of the people. Hezekiah's own son, Manasseh, quickly reversed all the good that his father had done. In less than a century the nation faced a new and more formidable threat from Nebuchadnezzar of Babylon.

Israel During the Time of Micah

The northern kingdom of Israel declined rapidly after the glory days of Jeroboam II (2 Kings 14:23–29). The chaotic political situation came about as a result of pressure from the Assyrian empire, with pro-Assyrian and anti-Assyrian parties within the country vying for power. During this period four kings were assassinated, there was a time when two kings were reigning at the same time (one in Samaria and the other in Gilead), and the last king was captured by Assyria. In a desperate bid to ward off Assyrian inroads into the country, Israel joined with a coalition of nations, including Aram, to meet the Assyrian army. When Israel and Aram were unable to persuade Judah to join the coalition, they attacked the sister nation. That venture failed when the Assyrian Tiglath-Pileser III entered the country at the bidding of Ahaz of Judah. Eventually Israel fell victim to the Assyrian army when Samaria was captured in 722 B.C.

The religious situation in Israel really began with Jeroboam I (930–910 B.C.), who set up the golden calves at Bethel and Dan, an act that greatly displeased the Lord (1 Kings 12:31–33; 15:34). Later Ahab (874–853 B.C.) introduced Phoenician elements into the worship of Israel. These included a temple and an altar for Baal at Samaria (1 Kings 16:32), an "Asherah" (1 Kings 16:33),[8] and permission for the activity of the "prophets of Baal" and "the prophets of Asherah" (1 Kings 18:19). Eventually the "practices of the house of Ahab" came to symbolize the evil that the Lord found in Israel (2 Kings 8:27; Mic. 6:16).

Even though Micah was from Judah and seems to have prophesied only there, he was commissioned by the Lord to preach against the entire nation, north and south (Mic. 1:5). In fact, Micah uses the term "Israel" twelve times, and in all but one or two (1:13–14) he means the whole nation, not merely the northern kingdom. Judah's guilt was even measured by the standard of Israel; the southern nation followed the same wicked practices of her northern sister (Mic. 6:16).

Micah in Relation to Isaiah

It is clear from the heading to Isaiah (1:1) that Micah and

Isaiah must have overlapped as contemporaries to some extent. They also have many similarities in content. Micah 4:1–4 closely parallels Isaiah 2:1–5, with much of the wording an exact match. Both prophets also foretell the Babylonian captivity, and both speak of the birth of the Messiah. In addition, they both address some of the same social and spiritual conditions.

Neither prophet records, however, any specific knowledge or awareness of the other. Isaiah is the more prominent of the two in the historical books. He receives direct mention in 2 Kings and in 2 Chronicles. Micah's name appears elsewhere in the Bible only in the book of Jeremiah (26:18), though he is quoted in the New Testament (see Matt. 2:6). Perhaps these facts can be explained in light of Isaiah's easy access to the king (see Isa. 7:3; 37:2). It may be as well that Micah's ministry ended around the time that Samaria fell (722 B.C.) and before Hezekiah's sole reign began.

Micah, however, was aware of another important part of the history of his country. Ever since the days of Moses, the Lord had raised up prophets to lead the people back to true worship. Samuel was a great man of God, and the Lord "let none of his words fall to the ground" (1 Sam. 3:19). Then there was Nathan, who gave the Lord's assurance to David that his dynasty and kingdom would endure forever (2 Sam. 7:11b–16). There were also Elijah and Elisha, who caused many in the north to reevaluate their ways and follow the Lord (1 Kings 17–2 Kings 13). Two other northern prophets, Jonah and Amos, were before Micah, and it is likely that he knew of them.

At some point in Micah's life the Lord laid a call upon him also to declare the prophetic word to the people. If Joel and Obadiah are placed after Micah chronologically, then Isaiah and Micah are the earliest of the writing prophets of Judah.

The Literary Characteristics of Micah's Book

All of Micah's book, with the exception of the heading (1:1), has been arranged as poetry by the modern versions. The beauty of his poetry when read aloud in the original Hebrew is almost impossible to duplicate in translation, but the reader of a good English version such as the NIV can well appreciate the tight parallelisms (see 1:2) and vivid images that abound in the book (see 1:4, 8). Also, a Bible with convenient marginal notations can enable the reader to experience some of the verbal force of various plays on words or sound associations that Micah excelled at so much (see below on 1:10–15). His ability to capture the essence of a difficult concept in a few memorable words is especially evident at 2:11; 5:2; 6:6–8; and 7:18–20.

THE MESSAGE OF MICAH FOR TODAY

As with all of the writing prophets, Micah has a strong sense of the need for justice in society, whether it be through the proper administration of justice in the courts (3:11; 7:3), through fairness in the marketplace (6:10–11), or through dealing with authority and power in a responsible manner (2:1–2, 8–9; 3:1–3, 9–10; 6:12; 7:2–6). He views this need for justice primarily through the perspective of the relationships that exist among people: rich to poor; prophets and priests to the laity; the powerful to the powerless; rulers to the people; a neighbor to a friend; and the members of a family to each other. The primary relationship which determines all the others, though, is that of the individual with his or her God (6:8). Since justice and mercy are the Lord's requirements, "to walk humbly with" Him must entail also fair dealings with others; and what is fair can be measured against the standard of what God has already "showed" humankind to be "good."[9] This issue of "social justice" brings Micah alive as a prophet who has much to say to all generations, including our own.

Another key theme in Micah of great contemporary relevance is that of the proper worship of the Lord. Like Amos, Micah deplores a religious system that has lots of ritual but little repentance. Here again his admonition "to walk humbly with . . . God" (6:8) brings forward the need for a total commitment of one's life to the Lord as the central issue. At the same time, Micah does not ignore the worship of other gods (1:6–7; 5:13) or of anything else that might become the main source of confidence for the believer other than the Lord (5:10–12).

Micah's teachings are in complete agreement with those of the Apostle Paul in this regard, who commanded all believers "to offer your bodies as living sacrifices, holy and pleasing to God" (Rom. 12:1).

Finally, even though Micah spent a lot of time preaching about judgment to come (also a topic of present-day relevance), he is above all a prophet of considerable hope for the future. His prophecy of the birth of the Messiah in Bethlehem was fulfilled in the birth of Jesus Christ more than 700 years later (Matt. 2:1–8; Luke 2:1–7), and that in itself gives confidence to believe that God will fulfill all of His promises to the believer. Micah gives much more detail about the coming kingdom of God and its blessings for the entire world. In the final chapter of his book, Micah shows himself to be a person who trusts that the Lord will accomplish His purposes in the world even when society is filled with corruption and violence. In this he is a model for the people of God in any age.

Structure and Outline

Feinberg, on the basis of Micah's call for the people to "hear" or "listen" to the Lord's message (1:2; 3:1; 6:1), divides the book into three parts: 1:1–2:13; 3:1–5:15; and 6:1–7:20.[10] While the summons to hear the Lord's word is an important organizing principle, the tripartite structure misses the significant fact that chapters 2 and 3 are united in the way they detail the sins of the leaders and the people, whereas chapters 4 and 5 are separated from the previous section by their common focus on the Lord's restoration. Mays found only "two major parts" to the book: 1:1–5:15 and 6:1–7:20.[11] Under this pattern both parts would include the topics of God's wrath and judgment, the sins of the people, and God's plan for restoration and forgiveness. The following outline stresses the concentration of these primary themes in certain sections of the book.

- I. Judgment for Israel and Judah (1:1–3:12)
  - A. Heading (1:1)
  - B. The Lord Comes to Judge the World (1:2–4)
    1. He Summons the Whole Earth to the Judgment (1:2)
    2. He Descends to the Earth in Power and Glory (1:3–4)
  - C. The Lord Comes to Judge Samaria and Judah (1:5–16)
    1. The Guilty Nations (1:5)
    2. The Sentence Against Samaria (1:6–7)
    3. The Sentence Against Judah (1:8–16)
  - D. The Lord Makes the Charges Against His People (2:1–13)
    1. Unlawful Seizure of Property (2:1–5)
    2. Failure to Recognize the Truth (2:6–13)
  - E. The Lord Rebukes the Leaders of His People (3:1–12)
    1. Because the Leaders Do Not Care for the People (3:1–4)
    2. Because the Prophets Give Them False Hope (3:5–8)
    3. Because the Leaders Pervert Everything That Is Right (3:9–12)
- II. Restoration in the Last Days (4:1–5:15)
  - A. Learning the Ways of the Lord at Jerusalem (4:1–5)
    1. The Highest Mountain (4:1a–b)
    2. All the Nations (4:1c)
    3. Instruction in Righteousness (4:2)
    4. The Lord as the Judge (4:3a)
    5. Peace on Earth (4:3b–4)
    6. The Name of the Lord Our God (4:5)
  - B. Restoration of the Scattered Remnant (4:6–7)
  - C. Restoration of the Kingship (4:8–5:6)
    1. The Kingship to Be Restored (4:8)
    2. Israel Without a King (4:9–10)
    3. The Plans of the Lord Versus the Plans of the Nations (4:11–13)
    4. The Rise of a New Ruler (5:1–6)

- D. Lifting Up the Remnant to Triumph Over Its Enemies 5:7–9)
- E. Everything Contrary to the Lord Destroyed from the Land (5:10–15)

III. The Lord's Complaint Against His People (6:1–16)
- A. The Case Against the People (6:1–12)
  1. God's Complaint Witnessed by the Mountains and Hills (6:1–2)
  2. God's Complaint in Light of His Past Treatment of Israel (6:3–5)
  3. God's Complaint Demonstrated by Their Religious Practices (6:6–7)
  4. God's Complaint in Light of What He Really Desires (6:8)
  5. God's Complaint Demonstrated by Their Injustice (6:9–12)
- B. The Punishment for the People (6:13–16)

IV. The Hope of the Godly (7:1–20)
- A. The Circumstances That Might Cause Despair (7:1–7)
  1. The Disappearance of the Godly from the Land (7:1–4a)
  2. The Judgment of God on the People (7:4b)
  3. The Breakdown of Relationships in Society (7:5–6)
  4. The Confidence of One Who Trusts in the Lord (7:7)
- B. The City That Will Be Victorious (7:8–13)
- C. The God Who Makes Hope Possible (7:14–20)
  1. The Prophet Prays for Restoration (7:14)
  2. The Lord Promises a New Deliverance (7:15)
  3. The Nations React to the Lord's Miracles (7:16–17)
  4. The People Trust in the Lord's Mercy (7:18–20)

12

JUDGMENT FOR ISRAEL AND JUDAH

MICAH 1:1–3:12

HEADING (1:1)

In common with the other prophets, Micah's book has a heading which was added to give the reader essential information. The authority of Micah to speak for the Lord is stressed by a twofold statement. "The word of the Lord" came to the prophet Micah, and he received it as a prophetic vision. The text says literally that Micah "saw" the Lord's word ("the vision"). This does not necessarily imply a visual mode of revelation; it can indicate prophetic revelation in general (see Isa. 2:1; 30:10; Ezek. 12:27). In noun form the same root means a "seer" (see Amos 7:12), and the verb used in the heading to a prophetic book would be a technical term to make the fact of divine inspiration clear.

Micah's heading also tells the reader the name of his hometown, Moresheth (also Moresheth Gath, Micah 1:14). It was located in the Judean foothills or "Shephelah," a small village not far from the town of Gath and about six miles northeast of Lachish. For a discussion of the kings mentioned in the heading, see the "Introduction."

The prophecy concerns Samaria and Jerusalem, the capital cities of Israel and Judah, respectively. The cities stand for their countries, so the prophecy really treats the entire nation, both north and south.

The Lord Comes to Judge the World (1:2–4)

In the first part of his book, Micah begins with a general statement that the Lord is coming to the earth to judge the whole world. Micah stresses the awesome power of the Lord and the comprehensiveness of His judgment.

He Summons the Whole Earth to the Judgment (1:2)

Micah's opening scene gives the reader a glimpse of the Lord descending to the earth in all of His power and might. As a result, the earth itself dissolves before Him. What judgment is Micah talking about here? Is he describing poetically the Assyrian invasions of Samaria and Judah, or is he speaking of a more universal judgment? Some think that when he summons the nations and the inhabitants of the earth (v. 2), he is calling them as witnesses, not as those who receive the judgment.[12] Micah says, however, "that the Sovereign Lord may witness against you," not "to you" or "before you." So *all the nations,* as shown by "all who are in [the earth]," will receive this judgment. Other prophecies also make it clear that great changes in the earth like Micah mentions (v. 4) will happen at the final judgment associated with the "day of the Lord" (see Isa. 13:9–13; Joel 3:15–16; Zech. 14:1–5).

He Descends to the Earth in Power and Glory (1:3–4)

This final judgment will demonstrate the power and justice of the Lord in a spectacular manner, and Micah joins it with the coming Assyrian invasion in order to impress on his audience the character of their God, who is sovereign over them. Just as surely as the Lord has the ability to melt the very elements of the earth, even so He has the sovereign power to direct the might of Assyria against Samaria and Judah. Leslie Allen compares Micah here with Amos 1–2, where Amos starts with the acceptable message that the Lord is judge of all the earth before he introduces the application to Israel itself.[13]

The "holy temple" from which the Lord bears testimony

against the nations (v. 2) parallels the "dwelling place" from which He comes to the earth (v. 3). Both expressions refer to the heavenly abode of the Lord (see also Ps. 11:4; Amos 9:6; Zech. 2:13).

The expression "high places of the earth" refers to the ridges of the mountains, but it also carries with it the connotation of the "high places" where the people worshiped their idols. By using terms with such emotive meaning, Micah foreshadows also the Lord's judgment against idolatry (1:7). The imagery of mountains melting and valleys splitting apart arouses emotions of awe and terror in the reader. Similar language occurs in Habakkuk 3:4–15, only there it speaks figuratively of the Lord coming forth to deliver His people.

The Lord Comes to Judge Samaria and Judah (1:5–16)

Suddenly Micah changes the focus of his message in a way that must have startled the Judeans. He states that the Lord's judgment will actually begin with His own people Israel. Both parts of the nation, represented by the capital cities of Samaria and Jerusalem, have transgressed against the Lord, and this will lead to the destruction of Samaria and the cities of Judah. After announcing the form of the judgment, Micah turns to the specific sins of the people (chap. 2), and finally he makes accusations against the rulers of the people (chap. 3).

The Guilty Nations (1:5)

At 1:5 Micah turns from the general judgment against the nations to the specific judgments against Samaria and Judah. "All this," Micah says, "is because of Jacob's transgression, because of the sins of the house of Israel." Up to this point Micah's listeners might have felt that God's own people were exempt, but Micah turns it around completely. Everything he has been talking about is because of Israel. The nations are of course guilty as well; Micah's "all" does not deny that. What Micah means is that even if the sins of Israel alone are considered and the guilt of the nations is ignored, God would still be justified to come to the land and judge the people so severely.

The referent of the term "Israel" is not always the same in the Old Testament. The patriarch Jacob was given the name Israel (Gen. 32:28), and his twelve sons became the twelve tribes of Israel.[14] Regularly in 1 and 2 Kings and sometimes in 1 and 2 Chronicles, "Israel" refers to the northern kingdom, while "Judah" is used for the southern kingdom. Hosea and Amos, who focused on the northern kingdom, sometimes use "Jacob" or "Israel" to refer to that kingdom (see Hos. 1:4, 11; 7:1; 10:11; 12:2; Amos 2:6; 3:13; 4:5; 5:1–2; 6:8; 7:2, 5). Even they, however, occasionally use "Israel" in relation to the entire people of God (see Hos. 1:10; 11:1; Amos 3:1). Isaiah, who lived during the divided monarchy and focused on Judah, tends to use "Israel" or "Jacob" for the whole people included in the twelve tribes (see 1:3; 2:5), except when he needs to stress the historical division (see 7:1). Micah oriented himself to the southern kingdom, but his prophecies include both north and south in a general way. In any event, Micah's references to "Israel" (except 1:13–14) and to "Jacob" should be taken with reference to the entire people, regardless of whether they are part of the southern or of the northern kingdom. To specify the northern kingdom, he uses "Samaria," its capital city, and for the south he uses either "Judah" or "Jerusalem."

Micah does not identify "Jacob" with the northern kingdom, as it might appear at first glance from 1:5. Rather, he states that Samaria became a source of transgression or sin for the entire people of God, and in the same way Jerusalem in Judah followed Samaria's example. Both kingdoms are equally guilty of corrupting the people of Israel or Jacob.

The Sentence Against Samaria (1:6–7)

The Lord revealed through Micah that He was planning to destroy Samaria completely. We know that this happened in 722 B.C. when the Assyrian army overran the city. As a result, the entire northern kingdom was incorporated into the Assyrian empire (see 2 Kings 17).[15]

The reader may well wonder what would cause such a passionate outburst against Samaria as is found in Micah 1:6–7. Micah focuses on the idolatry of the northern kingdom, singling out especially the places of worship and the idols that had angered the Lord so much. In Old Testament times Samaria was a city situated on a high hill,[16] and it is easy to imagine that the invaders hurled all the contents of the city into the valley below.

Micah also mentions Samaria's "gifts from the wages of prostitutes" (1:7). The city was quite wealthy and prosperous, a result of corruption and greed as well as trade and relations with other nations, such as Egypt and Phoenicia. Numerous ivory plaques and fragments, some of them probably dating from the eighth century B.C., have been discovered through archaeological investigation at Samaria. Avigad explains their presence: "The ivories are considered as products of Phoenician art, and they were probably used as inlays in the palace furniture of the Israelite kings."[17] Micah evidently means in a figurative sense that the nation of Israel committed spiritual adultery against the Lord by embracing the idolatrous religions of their trading partners and allies (compare Hosea). It also may have been fairly common for young Israelite women and men to participate in temple prostitution as part of the rites associated with the fertility goddess (see Hos. 4:14). Micah summarized well how appropriate Samaria's punishment would be: "Since she gathered her gifts from the wages of prostitutes, as the wages of prostitutes they will again be used." Perhaps one could think, with Allen, of the soldiers tearing down the images and using the precious materials on them for hiring their own prostitutes.[18]

The Sentence Against Judah (1:8–16)

The wound which proved to be fatal to Samaria, Micah laments, "has reached the very gate of my people, even to Jerusalem itself" (1:9). In this way Micah turns his attention to Judah and Jerusalem, the focal points of the remainder of his book. The southern kingdom will not escape the Lord's hand of judgment, for the people of Judah have become just as guilty as their northern neighbors in their rebellion against the Lord (see 1:13).

Micah describes in startling terms his own process of grieving for what will happen to the nation. Leslie Allen has a pertinent comment:

> For most of us mourning is traditionally a quiet affair symbolized by drawn curtains and the declining of invitations, but for the Israelite it was a matter of noisy expression of one's anguish. The more keenly felt the bereavement, the louder the shrieking.[19]

So Micah speaks of wandering about "barefoot and naked," howling and moaning because of the fate of the people. This would dramatically illustrate the grave consequences of the path God's people were currently walking.

Micah turns his attention from Jerusalem to eleven towns in the Shephelah or low hill country of Judah between the coastal plain on the west and the higher mountains on the east (1:10–15). From his hometown of Moresheth Gath, Micah was able to look out over the low hills of the Shephelah and think about these towns and cities. He could also lift his eyes to the mountains of Judah on the east and pick out the point where Jerusalem would be (about twenty miles to the northeast). Then he could turn his eyes northeastward toward Samaria and the hill country of Ephraim.

As he saw the land that encompassed Israel and Judah, surely the history of the two nations must have come to his mind. He would have been familiar with the traditions that had been passed down, and especially with the Law of Moses. He would have known that these two nations had once worshiped Yahweh together as one people. They had recognized Him as the Creator of heaven and earth. Micah would also have known about the time when great leaders like Deborah, Barak, Gideon, and Samson had arisen to turn the people back to the Lord when they had strayed after the idols of the Canaanite people. That time, in turn, was followed by the rise of the united monarchy under Saul, David, and Solomon.

Micah's heart must have been heavy when he thought about the time after Solomon when the country split into two parts, with one king for the north and one for the south. Ever since, there had been a division which caused a rift not only between the people, but also between the people and their God. Looking up to the mountains that run through the middle of Israel from north to south, Micah could see the area that served as a dividing line between the two countries.

In Micah's own time, late in the reign of Jotham and early in the reign of Ahaz, the divisions between Israel and Judah boiled over into war. A number of countries in that part of the Fertile Crescent which extends between the Euphrates in the north and Egypt in the south decided to form an alliance to defy growing Assyrian power. Aram (Syria) and Israel (Ephraim) were two leading countries in this coalition. The Assyrians were demanding tribute from the Western countries and trying to dominate the trade routes that led northward from Egypt. King Ahaz of Judah saw the political folly in such a move and refused to join the coalition. As a result, Aram and Israel attacked Judah, and Ahaz called on Assyria for help. The powerful Tiglath-Pileser III defeated the coalition, at the same time incorporating Aram into the Assyrian empire and installing a puppet king over Israel (2 Kings 16:1–9; 2 Chron. 28:5–21; Isa. 7:1–9).[20] The pro-Assyrian stance of Ahaz likely had a lot of opposition in Judah, and one writer thinks that the cities of the Shephelah of Judah mentioned in Micah 1:10–15 actually sided with the coalition against their own king.[21]

Micah was also aware that the idolatry and false worship that had infected the northern kingdom so strongly was now making significant inroads into his own country. He could see that the cancer already had reached "the very gate of my people, even to Jerusalem itself" (Mic. 1:9).

About six miles southeast of his own town, Micah could see the imposing hill upon which the great and ancient city of Lachish sat. Two major highways intersected at Lachish, and it was a city of great wealth and strategic importance. From there it was possible to travel east to Hebron, north to Gath, northeast to Azekah, and southwest to connections that eventually led to Egypt. The road to Azekah passed right by Micah's hometown.

Micah noticed something more ominous about Lachish than its impressive facade. He saw it as a source of idolatrous practices which spread from there to Jerusalem (Mic. 1:13). Such practices became rampant in Judah during the reign of Ahaz (see "Judah Under Ahaz" in the Introduction to the commentary).

The Lord revealed to Micah that the sins of Judah would lead to the nation's downfall, even as similar sins had caused the downfall of Israel. As Micah announces the Lord's judgment, he emphasizes Jerusalem and Lachish. Jerusalem is "the very gate of my people." That is, the city is the entrance into the hearts of the people.

Micah makes a pun or a play on words out of the name of each town as he describes the effects the disaster will have on it. This serves to reinforce the thought that each town deserves the punishment it will receive and that it is appropriate to the transgression. The following chart illustrates the details of the wordplays.

Name of Town	Comments	Play on Words
Gath (1:10)	The sound of "Gath" is similar to part of the sound of the Hebrew word for "tell" *(taggidu)*.	"In *Gath* do not *gad* about with the news."
Beth–le–aphrah (1:10) (Beth Ophrah, NIV)	"Aphrah" and "dust" *(aphar)* sound similar.	"In the House of *Dust* roll in the *dust*."
Shapir (1:11)	"Shaphir" means "beautiful," and "nakedness and shame" contrast with it.	"Pass on in nakedness and shame, you who live in Beautiful."
Zaanan (1:11)	The sound of the name is partly similar to the Hebrew word for "come out" *(yazeah)*.	"Those who live in *Come*-town will not *come* out."

Name of Town	Comments	Play on Words
Beth Ezel (1:11)	The root meaning of "Ezel" is "to take away." A synonym is used in the statement.	"The House of *Taking-Away* . . . its protection is taken."
Maroth (1:12)	The name sounds like a word meaning "bitter," and this contrasts with "relief," which also can mean "good" or "sweet."	"Those who live in *Bitter*-town . . . wait for something *sweet.*"
Lachish (1:13)	"Lachish" sounds like the Hebrew term for "team" *(rechesh).*	"You who live in *Lachish* harness a *rechesh*-team."
Moresheth Gath (1:14)	The root of "Moresheth" means "become engaged," and the term for "parting gifts" can also mean a "dowry."	"You will give a *dowry* for the *Fiancée*-of-Gath."
Aczib (1:14)	The name sounds similar to the Hebrew term for "deceptive" *(aczab).*	"The town of *Deceit* will prove *deceptive.*"
Mareshah (1:15)	The sound of the name is partly similar to the Hebrew term for "conqueror" *(yoresh).*	"I will bring a *con*-queror against you who live in *Con*-ville."
Adullam (1:15)	The sound of the name is partly similar to the Hebrew term for "to" *(ad).*	"He. . . will come to *To*-ville."

Why is it that Micah says not to tell about the judgment in Gath and not to weep there? The first part of his statement imitates the words of David's lament when Saul was slain: "Tell it not in Gath" (2 Sam. 1:20). Saul had been slain by the Philistines, so David in his sorrow wished that there would not be rejoicing in the streets of the Philistine towns when the news was heard. Micah appears to have a similar idea in mind; he wishes there was no good news for the enemies of Judah to hear. Also, when the mourner says a lament, the news is heard by all those around. So the statement, "Weep not at all."

The people of Shaphir will "pass on," perhaps as refugees or captives, humiliated and ashamed. That no one leaves Zaanan may mean either that none will survive the disaster or that they will be too afraid to come out and fight.[22] The inhabitants of Beth Ezel will mourn for the slain people they will not be able to protect. Those who live in Maroth will suffer extreme hardship as they wait for relief that cannot come because even Jerusalem will suffer. In Lachish the people will try to escape in chariots or to mount a counterattack. Either way the implication is that it will be a vain effort.

What happens to Moresheth Gath, according to 1:14? If Moresheth Gath receives a dowry ("parting gifts"), then she is promised to a husband. That is, "she is doomed to come under the jurisdiction of the enemy invader."[23] The dowry would then be "an indemnity to be paid in addition to the loss of the town."[24]

Evidently the population of Aczib would see the disaster coming and hastily change sides in a last attempt to avoid it.[25] Do the people deceive the kings of the northern kingdom of Israel? If so, when? Or, do they betray the monarchy,[26] denying that they have any king, whether of Israel or of Judah? The answers are not clear from the text. Mareshah was also a fortified city of the Shephelah (2 Chron. 11:8).

Finally, Micah states, "He who is the glory of Israel will come to Adullam." In light of the entire context, it does not seem that the prophet means something positive by this. It cannot be a reference to the Lord or to the Messiah. David hid with his men from Saul in a large cave near Adullam (1 Sam. 22:1; 2 Sam. 23:13), and it may be that Micah intends the reader to recall that incident. Even as David had to hide in the cave, so all the aristocracy in the Shephelah area or throughout all Israel (north and south) would be forced to flee and hide.[27] The line could be paraphrased, "The nobility of Israel will flee to Adullam to hide."[28]

What was the disaster that Micah foresaw would happen to Judah? There is much to be said in favor of the view that he was referring to the future invasion of Judah by Sennacherib, the king of Assyria. First, the author of 2 Kings states that "Sennacherib king of Assyria attacked all the fortified cities of Judah and captured them" (2 Kings 18:13). Sennacherib's own inscription mentions forty-six fortified cities and walled forts in Hezekiah's country that he conquered.[29] It makes sense militarily that the towns of the Shephelah would be among the first in Judah to fall. Indeed, Sennacherib made the city of Lachish, mentioned in Micah 1:13, the center of his operations in Judah (2 Kings 18:17). Second, the elders in Jeremiah's day quoted Micah 3:12 in relation to the destruction of Jerusalem, noting that in Micah's own day the Lord spared the city because the people repented (Jer. 26:18). They were referring to how the angel of the Lord killed 185,000 of Sennacherib's soldiers in a single night, causing the Assyrian king to make a hasty retreat to Nineveh (2 Kings 19:35–36).

Actually, Micah does not mention Assyria by name or any Assyrian king in the first chapter. While Sennacherib's invasion fulfills many of the details, the prophecy is vague enough that an earlier Assyrian incursion or even later invasions by the Babylonians could meet the intent of the prophecy. Also, it should be mentioned that the things that Micah said about each city need not be restricted to that city only. It would be expected that in a general invasion there would be many in all of the cities who would flee or mourn or betray their nation. The requirements of the poetry dictated which action went with which city or town.

Micah began this section by expressing his own grief. At the conclusion (1:16) he calls on the people of Judah to grieve for the children they will lose in the invasion, whether to death or to exile. To shave the hair was a sign of deep mourning and grief (Isa. 15:2; Jer. 16:6; Amos 8:10).[30]

The Lord Makes the Charges Against His People (2:1–13)

After Micah lays out the judgment from the Lord that was

about to happen to Israel and Judah, he turns to some of the specific charges against God's people. In chapter 2 these charges are made with respect to the people in general, while in chapter 3 the leaders of the people are rebuked for their role in what has happened. Micah talks about false prophets in both chapters, but in chapter 2 he focuses on why the prophecies they are making are false. It is because they are saying that the Lord will not bring judgment, even though the people have become violent and oppressive against the helpless. The last part of chapter 2 (vv. 12–13) contains a positive note of restoration, but that positive message needs to be seen against the background of the false prophecies. It is false to say that the Lord will not punish the people when they do wrong. It is true, however, to speak of the Lord's faithfulness despite the faithlessness of the people. The judgment will refine the people so that only a righteous remnant remains; and the Lord will gather that remnant and will once again bless them in the land, in accordance with His numerous promises.

Unlawful Seizure of Property (2:1–5)

Micah proclaims the Lord's word in a very vivid and straightforward manner. He brings us into the bedrooms of those who covet their neighbors' property so much that they spend most of the night coming up with a plan and rise at dawn to carry it out. Having done so, "they defraud a man of his home, a fellowman of his inheritance" (2:2b). This is in direct violation of the tenth commandment (Ex. 20:17), which uses the same Hebrew term for "covet" as found in Micah 2:2.

Who was guilty of these sins that Micah describes? We know from Amos that such practices were characteristic of the northern kingdom (Amos 2:6–7; 5:11; 8:4–6), but Isaiah also observed similar oppressions in Judah (Isa. 5:8). Since Micah focuses mostly on Judah (see 1:9–16; 3:9–10; 5:2), it seems best to apply his descriptions to the land barons of the southern kingdom. Certainly, though, the words could apply to either nation.

In order to understand why the Lord considered unlawful

seizure of property such a severe sin, it will be helpful to survey what it meant to have property in ancient Israel. The Mosaic law made provision for extended families to receive the right to derive a livelihood from certain portions of the land (Num. 33:50–54). In a theological sense, the Lord owns the land, but he allowed families to actually control the different plots. These tracts of land were to remain within the families perpetually; they could not be bought and sold permanently. During the year of Jubilee all land was to be restored to its rightful condition whenever individuals did get displaced (Lev. 25:23–28).[31]

Micah returns to the theme of the Lord's judgment on the people for their sins in 2:3–5, but this time he phrases the sentence to reflect the appropriateness of the punishment for unlawful seizure of land. The people who coveted more land and thought nothing of taking from others what they wanted will find themselves destitute of any possessions, and the invaders who seize their land will ridicule and taunt them. The newly impoverished Judeans will be forced to listen to their own lament thrown back in their faces: "We are utterly ruined."

Verse 5 makes reference back to the way land was periodically reallocated by lot in Israel. This was a part of the year of Jubilee, but may have happened on other occasions as well. Allen refers to Psalm 16:6 as a parallel:[32]

> The boundary lines have fallen for me in pleasant places;
> surely I have a delightful inheritance.

Perhaps the scheming that the evildoers did on their beds concerned a way to manipulate or circumvent the redistribution process. In the future restoration of the people to their land (2:12–13), those who sought to gratify their own covetous desires will not be able to take part. This is in line with the teaching of the Lord Jesus Christ that in seeking to gain life it is lost, but in losing one's life it is found (Matt. 16:25–26).

Failure to Recognize the Truth (2:6–13)

Whenever there are those who carry out the Lord's ministry,

there are usually those who minister under false pretenses and give a false message. Micah and Isaiah received a genuine call from the Lord to preach His message to the people, but there were also many false prophets. One major characteristic of a false prophet is that he preaches only positive messages and leaves out the negative words of judgment (compare 1 Kings 22:6–28, 37–38). At this point Micah concentrates on the failure of the message of these prophets to measure up to the truth. Later, in 3:5, he points out also their lack of moral character.

The lie of the false prophets is simply this: "Disgrace will not overtake us" (2:6). They justify their error with false theology, implying with rhetorical questions that the Lord does not act in the angry way that Micah has described (2:7a). The Lord's reply through Micah is that it is true that He promises ("my words")[33] to bless ("good"), but only "to him whose ways are upright" (2:7b). So Micah brings the question back to the real issue. It is not whether the Lord can or cannot bring judgment, but whether or not the people deserve it.

The people have "risen up like an enemy" (2:8a). The text does not make it clear if they act like enemies to the Lord or to other people. The context supports the first idea. They have become the Lord's enemies because they mistreat others. Their behavior is inconsistent with any sense in which they might be considered God's people.

Micah gives concrete instances of how the people show their hostility toward God (2:8b–9). Enemies usually fight wars. Even so these people act like soldiers who are returning from a war. They lie in wait for innocent passersby and strip off their clothes;[34] they drive widows out of their houses; and they deprive the children of any real future. The phrase "my blessing" is literally "my splendor," and it is not clear exactly what is meant. It probably refers in a general way to all that the Lord desires to give the children in the future.[35] Actual soldiers would do these things by physical force, but it may be that Micah has in mind a more figurative sense. Some are oppressing the people by abuse of political power in such a way that they are accomplishing the same ends that violent means would accomplish. If so, then Micah's statements would be more in line with the oppressions described by the prophet Amos for the northern kingdom (see Amos 2:6–8; 5:11; 6:1–7; 8:5–6).

The Lord commands such ruthless people to leave the land because they have defiled it by their crimes (2:10). They will exit the land in only one of two ways: either by captivity or by death.

Micah returns to the theme of false prophecy in 2:11. Here, though, he speaks in a highly ironic tone. If a prophet comes along who will tell the oppressors they will have all the "wine and beer" they desire, he will be perfect for them. That is, they would hear what they wanted to hear, and the truth could not give them any opportunity to escape.

In fact, the Lord does plan to bless His people, but only in the future after He has refined them through the disaster. The language of 2:12–13 is consistent with the future restoration of Israel to their land in the millennial kingdom.[36] The features that indicate this are: (1) the reuniting of Israel and Judah (see Isa. 11:12–13; Ezek. 37:15–28; Hos. 1:11; Obad. 17–20); (2) the spilling over of the population into the countryside (see Hos. 1:10; Zech. 2:4–5); and (3) the direct leadership of the Lord as King over His people (see Isa. 2:2–4; Mic. 4:2–3; Zech. 14:9). According to Feinberg, "This is none other than the Messiah of Israel who breaks down every obstacle in the path of His people."[37]

The Lord Rebukes the Leaders of His People (3:1–12)

Judah and Israel had three categories of leaders: rulers, prophets, and priests. The term "rulers" in 3:1 and 9 refers to political leaders,[38] especially the king and elders. These had a responsibility to maintain justice in the land, justice being defined by the Lord Himself. The prophets were supposed to tell the people whatever message the Lord wanted them to hear, and that was often with regard to how the people or their leaders were violating the Lord's will. The priests had the task of teaching the people how God's law applied to specific situations. Each of these three areas of leadership, then, was supposed to be informed by the will of the Lord.

Micah's complaints in chapter 3 focus on exactly the issue of the ultimate source of the national leadership. The rulers do not care for the people; they are interested only in benefiting themselves (3:2–3). Likewise the prophets are saying what the people want to hear, not what God has told them to say. They will not give any message that does not motivate the people to give them food (3:5). For the sake of what they can get from it, all of the leaders "distort all that is right" (3:9).

Because the Leaders Do Not Care for the People (3:1–4)

In 3:1–2, Micah uses a vivid figure for what is happening. It might at first glance seem to be even cannibalistic, but probably Micah views the people as sheep and the leaders as their shepherds (see Ezek. 34:2–4 and Zech. 11:16–17). These leaders had perverted the Lord's justice to the point where they "hate good and love evil." As a consequence, the flock became only dinner on the table of their shepherds; there was no sense of compassion or of helping others.

When the leaders of God's people take advantage of the people in such a vicious manner, they cannot expect to receive any help from the Lord when they in turn are in trouble (3:4). They may cry out to the Lord for deliverance, but "he will hide his face from them." Micah is evidently thinking of the invasion of the country he mentioned previously (1:10–16; 2:3–5).

Because the Prophets Give Them False Hope (3:5–8)

Likewise, during this invasion the false prophets will be of no value: "They will all cover their faces because there is no answer from God" (3:7). Habitual liars will not be able to find truth when they need it. Instead of telling a message they received from the Lord, they shaped their message according to how the people fed them (3:5). Such behavior was not in any way typical of a true prophet (see 2 Kings 5:15–27; Amos 7:12–15). Micah also makes two references to divination in verses 6–7,[39] a practice of which the Lord strongly disapproved (Deut. 18:10; 1 Sam. 15:23; 2 Kings 17:17; Isa. 44:25). This gives another indication that these were false prophets.

By contrast, Micah tells the people that his message comes from the Lord (3:8). He does not bear a word that is easy to hear; it concerns transgressions and sins against God. It is a message, however, that he has received from the Lord Himself.

Micah enumerates four ways in which he differs from the political and religious leaders of the day: He is "filled with power, with the Spirit of the Lord, and with justice and might" (3:8). All four of these represent characteristics of a true prophet that are closely interrelated. "Power" suggests the limitless power of God. He displayed His power in creation (Isa. 40:26; Jer. 10:12; 32:17) and when He brought Israel out of Egypt (Ex. 9:16; 15:3–6); He also displays it anytime He delivers His people (Isa. 40:29; 63:1).[40] Micah's message was different in that it had the source of its power in the Lord. It would be effective to accurately predict the future and to have an effect on the lives of those who heard it.

Any true prophet must have his inspiration through the Spirit of the Lord, and through His Spirit the Lord gives both revelation and power (1 Kings 18:12; 22:24; Neh. 9:30; Ezek. 11:5). The judges or charismatic leaders whom the Lord sent to deliver Israel in the period of the judges received their strength from the Lord's Spirit (Judg. 3:10; 6:34; 11:29; 13:25; 14:6, 19; 15:14). Likewise Saul and David, the first two kings of Israel, received their extraordinary ability to rule through the Spirit (1 Sam 10:6; 16:13). The same is true of the Messiah, portrayed in the Old Testament as the coming king who will rule the world in justice and righteousness (Isa. 11:2; 61:1). Actually, the Lord's power through His Spirit is available to any who trust confidently in Him (Isa. 40:28–31; Zech. 4:6). Micah's ministry was different because he worked through the power of the Spirit, instead of in his own human power.

Micah also speaks of being filled with "justice." Obviously the leaders of Israel had a different attitude toward justice; they despised it and distorted it (3:9). Whether something is just or not can only be judged by a standard, and only the Lord is capable of setting that standard. He revealed that standard through the Law of Moses, and that Law is summed up in two commandments: to love the Lord with all one's heart and to love one's neighbor as oneself (Deut. 6:4; see also Luke 10:27). The leaders showed their lack of justice by the way they treated the people. By their bloodshed, bribery, and stealing they revealed quite plainly their unjust ways. By contrast, Micah spoke out boldly on behalf of the oppressed and exposed unrighteousness. He was truly a prophet of justice.

Finally, Micah says he is filled with "might," a concept closely related to "power." The term "might" is sometimes associated with justice and righteousness as well as with God's Spirit (Pss. 65:5–6; 71:16; 89:13–14; Isa. 11:2; 63:14–15).[41] Micah's might derived from the Lord; that of the selfish leaders stemmed from their own abilities and cleverness. In their world "might makes right," but the Lord would bring a time when His might would overwhelm the power of the unrighteous and make things truly right in Israel.

Because the Leaders Pervert Everything That Is Right (3:9–12)

In the conclusion to chapter 3 (vv. 9–12), Micah repeats his call to the leaders to "hear" the Lord's message (see 3:1). In his summons he describes them in three ways. With regard to justice, they pervert it and ignore it. With regard to selfless leadership, they refuse to perform their "ministry" without a financial reward. With regard to the source of their message, they lend the Lord's name to their own opinion: "Is not the Lord among us? No disaster will come upon us" (3:11). Behavior like this, says Micah, will be the direct cause of the fall of Jerusalem (3:12).

It might be easy to misapply Micah's characterization of the leaders performing their services for money. He does not mean to imply that it is wrong for pastors, missionaries, or other types of ministers to receive financial support from those to whom they minister. Both the Old and the New Testaments fully support the concept that the Lord expects His people to provide for the needs of such workers (see Num. 18:21; Deut. 26:12; 1 Kings 17:7–16; 2 Kings 4:8–10; Neh. 10:38; Matt. 10:10; Luke 10:7; 1 Tim. 5:17–18).

Nevertheless, there are some important principles about financial support of Christian workers that can be derived from Micah's prophecy. First, the motive for doing the work must be to please the Lord. If it is for financial or material gain, then it is wrong. According to 3:5, the prophets actually geared their message according to what the people gave them. This comes out even more clearly with regard to the leaders who were rendering a judgment in court for a bribe (3:11). If the money influences the judgment, that is an injustice. Second, the fact that the priests were teaching "for a price" (3:11) must mean that they were demanding more than that to which they were actually entitled. This would in effect be taking advantage of the situation. A line between right and wrong is crossed when pastors make unreasonable demands based on their authority. This principle might also be applied to appeals for money that overstate the need, come too often, or misuse emotional appeal. Finally, the leaders in Micah's day, whether political or religious, were supposed to make sure that justice was done, especially in terms of helping the needy and protecting the helpless. Even so, church leaders of today should be concerned to see that the Lord's money is not spent extravagantly to satisfy the desires of a few at the expense of areas of real need.

13

RESTORATION IN THE LAST DAYS

MICAH 4:1–5:15

One of the marks of a true prophet of the Old Testament period was that he spoke of judgment against the Lord's people in response to their sinfulness. It is characteristic as well, though, that they had a message of hope and encouragement for the future of Israel. God's plan for His people is always full of hope and for their ultimate good (see Jer. 29:10–14; Rom. 8:28–30). The end or goal is to bring His people to a point of maturity, expressed in the Old Testament as having the Law written on their hearts (Jer. 31:33) and in the New Testament as being conformed to the likeness of Christ (Rom. 8:28). Judgment or punishment is only a means to that end.

Micah already gave a brief glimpse of the Lord's plans for the future in 2:12–13, but right at the heart of his book, in chapters 4 and 5, he lays out the details in a bold and stunning way. Micah's vision of the future seems almost to leap back and forth through history, jolting the reader at each turn. Consequently the section is difficult to organize, though it is tied together by the common theme of renewed hope for the future.

If we turn to the middle of the passage, we find the well-known prophecy of a new importance for lowly Bethlehem, because the future ruler of Israel, the Messiah, will come from there (5:2). Anytime that something of such great importance occurs at the center of a message, the reader should at least suspect a "chiastic" or "envelope" structure (see chap. 1 of the commentary). Such seems to be the case here, as outlined below.

Part 1a Learning the Ways of the Lord at Jerusalem (4:1–5)
  Part 2a Restoration of the Scattered Remnant (4:6–7)
    Center Restoration of the Kingship (4:8–5:6)
  Part 2b Lifting Up the Remnant in Triumph Over Its Enemies (5:7–9)
Part 1b Everything Contrary to the Lord Destroyed from the Land (5:10–15)

This structure begins and ends with the will of the Lord established in the land, and it focuses attention on the central role of the coming Messiah in His program.

Micah describes first the blessings of the kingdom of God on earth (4:1–5), focusing on the vital place of Jerusalem in that kingdom. Then he adds detail to how that will come about, starting with the Lord gathering a remnant from all those who have been driven away from the land of Israel (4:6–7). Next, Micah talks about how the Lord will restore the kingship to the people who will lose their independent status after the coming invasions (4:8–5:6). Returning to the issue of the remnant, he shows that the Lord will reverse the normal roles of exiles and their captors: the exiles will defeat the nations that hold them captive (5:7–9). Finally, Micah lets his readers know how the Lord will turn His judgment against Israel into something positive (5:10–15). Through it He will remove every vestige of support in which the people have trusted: military might; fortifications; magic or sorcery; and idols. Whatever it is that the people have trusted outside of the Lord Himself will perish. Only the Lord will be left, and that will be the point at which He will gather the exiles to the land, give them victory over their enemies, and reestablish His Law from Zion.

Learning the Ways of the Lord at Jerusalem (4:1–5)

Almost surprising in its abruptness,[42] Micah's short prophecy tells about the coming kingdom that places Jerusalem and the temple mount at the center of the world. Actually, it is the Lord who is central to the passage, but the nations will go up to Jerusalem to learn from Him there. The prophecy must come true, "for the Lord Almighty has spoken" (4:4).

Micah immediately sets the time frame for the fulfillment; it will happen "in the last days." There may be a deliberate reference here to Deuteronomy 4:30,[43] where Moses spoke of a time "in later days" when the people would return to the Lord and obey Him after a period of "distress" (see also Deut. 31:29; Jer. 23:20; 30:24; Hos. 3:5). An appeal to the instruction of Moses would validate Micah's message. Moses foresaw a time of great trouble for Israel due to her sins, followed by restoration when she repents. Micah simply adds detail to what the Lord has already revealed through Moses.

Some other events are connected to the phrase "in the last days." At that time the Lord will restore other nations besides Israel to their former greatness (Jer. 48:47; 49:39); the nations of the world will invade Israel (Ezek. 38:14–23; see also Zech. 14:1–5); and Daniel's vision of the end times will be fulfilled (Dan. 10:14). Joel uses a similar expression ("afterward") to refer to the time when the Lord will pour out His Spirit on all Israel (see comments on Joel 2:28). The New Testament writers use the phrase "last days" for either the age which began with the first coming of Christ (Acts 2:14–36, quoting from Joel 2:28; 1 Peter 1:20; Heb. 1:2) or the last part of this age when wickedness will increase in an unprecedented manner just prior to the second coming of Christ (2 Tim. 3:1; James 5:3; 2 Peter 3:3).

Micah's prophecy includes five elements, all of which have an important implication for the entire world:

1. The Lord's house will rise above all the surrounding mountains.
2. All the nations, not just Israel, will come to know and worship the Lord in Jerusalem.
3. Instructions in righteousness for the entire world will be issued from the Lord's house.
4. The Lord Himself will judge disputes among the nations.
5. True peace will prevail over the whole world.

The way that the Lord's work causes spiritual changes in the nations of the world as well as Israel indicates that Micah is referring to the coming of God's kingdom to the earth. From a New Testament perspective, this is the time of the Millennium that begins after the Rapture of the church and Christ's return to the earth in triumph (Rev. 19:11–20:6).

The Highest Mountain (4:1a–b)

Micah turns his focus first to the temple mount in Jerusalem. From the temple platform on top of this hill,[44] one overlooks valleys to the east, west, and south; but the mountains that surround the city are actually higher in elevation (see Ps. 125:2). In that future day, Micah prophesies, the temple mount will rise in elevation to tower over these other mountains.[45] There is a spiritual point to this change in elevation. The worship of the Lord in Jerusalem will become the central activity of the people. There seems also to be a physical aspect to the elevation, though, that is caused by great upheavals in the area (Zech. 14:3–5, 10–11).

All the Nations (4:1c)

Micah teaches in addition that "many nations" will go up to the Lord's mountain to learn what He requires of them. This gives the book a more universal appeal beyond Israel itself. In light of the invasion by a foreign nation that Micah foresaw (chap. 1), this universal perspective takes the reader by surprise. Micah presents here a stunning reversal. Israel was too corrupt for anything but destruction in war; but in the future she, along with all the nations, will become so steeped in the ways of righteousness that peace will break out everywhere in the world.

Other prophets share Micah's universal outlook. Isaiah, in addition to having in common with Micah the oracle of "the last days," speaks of Egypt, Assyria, and Israel worshiping the Lord together (19:23–25), of "all peoples" at a banquet that "the Lord Almighty will prepare" on the temple mount (25:6–8), and of "the islands" (or coastlands) putting their hope "in his law" (42:4). Amos knows of a "remnant of Edom and all the nations that bear my [God's] name" (9:12; compare Acts 15:12–21);[46] and the Lord sent Jonah on a mission to the hated and cruel Assyrians, the very instrument of God's punishment of the northern kingdom. Also Zechariah predicts that those among the nations who survive the Lord's judgment will go up to Jerusalem "year after year to worship the King, the Lord Almighty, and to celebrate the Feast of Tabernacles" (14:16).

INSTRUCTION IN RIGHTEOUSNESS (4:2)

"Walking" in biblical language often refers to behavior. To "walk" in the Lord's "ways" is to obey what He has commanded. The "ways" and "paths" of the Lord are always right; a person will never go wrong by walking in them. Waltke has an interesting comment on the terms "ways" and "paths":

> Here the word *ways* probably refers to the instructions in the law and *paths* to the prophetic word based on them (v. 2b).[47]

The nations need to have instruction in the Lord's ways, and that instruction comes from the "law" or the "word" of the Lord. Micah sees that the world will become what the Lord planned it to be, but quite contrary to what it was in his day. According to the Law of Moses, the people were to go to the priests for instruction in how to apply its laws to their everyday lives (Deut. 17:8–12; see also Mic. 3:11; Mal. 2:7), yet the priests were refusing to teach without extra money and were in any case perverting the law (3:9, 11). Even though the people of Israel were supposed to be "witnesses" to the fact that the Lord (Yahweh) is the only God (Isa. 44:8; see also Zech. 8:23), the nations could not see anything in Israel and Judah other than idolatry and its corrupt practices (1:7, 13).

According to Micah, the time will come when the nations of the world will go to Jerusalem to receive a true word of instruction from the Lord Himself. The Hebrew term for "law" also means "instruction," and its verb form means "to teach" or "to instruct." By combining the terms "teach" and "law" with "the word of the Lord," which often refers to prophetic instruction, Micah stresses the written word as it is properly taught.

THE LORD AS THE JUDGE (4:3A)

Judges have one of the most difficult jobs; it is seldom easy to sort out truth from error or to find the most equitable solution to a confusing situation. The Old Testament writers saw the judge as one who must be able to discern wisely and act in agreement with the just standards of the Lord (see Ex. 18:13–26; Deut. 1:16; 16:18). In addition, many cases arose which would be impossible or impractical for a human judge to decide. In such instances the disputing parties recognized that only the Lord could be entrusted with the proper judgment (Gen. 31:52; Judg. 11:27; 1 Sam. 24:11–15). In fact, for injustice on a worldwide scale, only the Lord can be counted on to one day make all things right (Pss. 82:8; 96:10; Joel 3:12).

The prophets viewed the fulfillment of the Lord's promise to one day establish justice on the earth in one of two ways. Either they saw a coming king, the Messiah, as the one who would judge the earth with fairness; or else they saw the Lord Himself acting directly in that role. These are not contradictory notions if it be remembered that the Messiah acts as the personal representative of the Lord (see Zech. 11:4–16; 13:7), to the extent that in some passages He is endowed with God's Spirit (Isa. 11:1–4) or even given titles or attributes that apply to God Himself (Pss. 45:6; 110:1; Isa. 9:6; Dan. 7:13–14). Often the prophets described the future kingdom in terms of both aspects, the Messiah as the King and the Lord Himself as the King (Isa. 7–11 and 33:17–22; Zech. 9:9–10 and 14:9). Micah designates the Lord as judge of the nations here, whereas in 5:2–5a he sees the Messiah who comes forth from Bethlehem as the one who will bring peace to the earth.

These two aspects of the Lord's future rule over the earth are blended neatly by the New Testament writers into the Lord Jesus Christ, both God and man, who will rule the earth with a rod of iron (Rev. 2:27; 12:5; 19:15; see also Ps. 2:9). Micah's picture of the future age, then, encompasses that time when all the nations will appear before the throne of Christ as He renders decisions that right all wrongs and settles disputes even between the nations.

PEACE ON EARTH (4:3B–4)

With the Lord Himself settling all disputes between the nations, war will at last become obsolete. On a worldwide scale the nations will turn their weapons into implements for peacetime activities. Soldiers will not even learn how to fight a war any longer; they will be too busy learning "the ways of the Lord" instead. This rather amazing state of affairs will happen not because of mutual respect and fear among the nations but because the Lord will directly intervene in the affairs of humankind. It can only happen "in the last days" when Jesus Christ returns to establish His kingdom on earth. As the "Prince of Peace" (Isa. 9:6), He will "proclaim peace" to the nations (Zech. 9:10).

The "vine" and the "fig tree" of 4:4 are symbols of the peacefulness and prosperity of the messianic era. The phrase was first applied to the reign of Solomon: "During Solomon's lifetime Judah and Israel, from Dan to Beersheba, lived in safety, each man under his own vine and fig tree" (1 Kings 4:25). Later the commander of the Assyrian troops took up the expression and proudly claimed that his king, Sennacherib, could provide that kind of security if the people of Jerusalem would only surrender to him (2 Kings 18:31; Isa. 36:16). Possibly Sennacherib's scribes got the wording from Micah (Isaiah did not use it in 2:2–5), or it may be that the language was traditional throughout the Near East. Zechariah, a prophet who ministered to the people of Judah who returned to their land from Babylonian captivity, used the expression in his vision about Joshua, the High Priest (Zech. 3:10). The point is that, because of external conditions in the world, the people will be able to enjoy the fruit of their labors in peace and security.

THE NAME OF THE LORD OUR GOD (4:5)

Micah concludes his glorious vision of the future with a statement of faith for the present. It might be years into the distant future before the prophecy is fulfilled, but however long it takes, those whose trust is in the Lord "will walk in the name of the Lord our God for ever and ever." Waltke calls this "a liturgical response" of "the faithful remnant."[48] It is a declaration, in any case, made despite whatever the other nations may be doing. Even if the Assyrians or the Babylonians or any other nation should overrun Israel and drive the people into exile, the Lord's faithful will always live their lives in tune with His will. In the future the nations will turn to Israel's God and learn of His ways, but it is enough for now that by faith those who have received the promise can look "forward to the city with foundations, whose architect and builder is God" (Heb. 11:10).

Restoration of the Scattered Remnant (4:6–7)

While 4:1–5 focused on the fact that Jerusalem would be the center of the Lord's worldwide kingdom, verses 6 and 7 bring into view the people who will survive the judgment of the Lord. The two sections are connected by the time frame: "In that day."

It is not clear from the English translation that the Lord views the people as sheep that have suffered in various ways. He plans to restore these distressed sheep to their land, where He will rule over them forever from Mount Zion.

Micah uses four terms to describe the afflicted of the people. First, they are "lame," just like their founding father Jacob, who walked with a limp after his encounter with God at Peniel (Gen. 32:31–32). The same rare Hebrew term for "lame" was used for both Jacob and the surviving people of Israel, even though a more common term was available. The only other place the word occurs is in Zephaniah 3:19, a passage which closely parallels Micah 4:6–7. The biblical writers viewed the lame, along with the deaf, the mute, and the blind, as those who would especially appreciate what the Lord would do for them in the messianic kingdom (see Isa. 35:6; Jer. 31:8). When Jesus Christ healed the lame and the blind, the deaf and the mute, it was taken as a sign that he was truly the Messiah (Matt. 11:2–6; Luke 7:20–23). Micah uses the term to imply that the whole nation that will go through the coming judgment of the Lord will be unable to enjoy the same independence and freedom that people with full use of their legs have.

The Hebrew term that the NIV translates with "exiles" could be taken as "those who have been scattered" (as in Jer. 40:12; 43:5; Zeph. 3:19). The people were exiles in a foreign country, of course, after they were scattered. Sheep tend to get into trouble when they are scattered.[49] They have no shepherd to rescue them, and more often than not they perish (contrast with Ezek. 34:15–16).

These sheep as well, the Lord says, are "those I have brought to grief." He is referring directly to the disastrous invasions of the land which will cause the flock to scatter in all directions. The prophets of the Old Testament are unanimous in the way they view the tragedy of the Assyrian and Babylonian conquests of Israel and Judah and the taking of the people into exile. To the ordinary observer it may look like the two tiny kingdoms were overrun by powerful world empires, but to the prophet who is granted God's perspective, the Lord creates history in such a way that it accomplishes His plans. So it is that the exile was a judgment with a purpose: to cause Israel to turn back to her God.

The final term for the people sums up the thought of scattering and disaster: "those driven away" (4:7). Here it is implied too that the Lord is the one who drove them away. In that future day, however, He will bring back the lame as a "remnant" and restore as a "strong nation" those He drove away or scattered. The Lord will "rule over" the people from Mount Zion, but the question of how He will do this is a question that is answered by the next major section.

RESTORATION OF THE KINGSHIP (4:8–5:6)

When the sheep are scattered, it is appropriate to ask about the shepherd, and that is precisely what Micah does next. In 4:8, Micah still refers to Israel as the "flock," reminding the readers of the scattered sheep that will be regathered, but raising, in addition, the issue of the shepherd. In this way the verse makes a transition to a new topic, the history of the kingship in Israel from the time of Micah to the time of the messianic kingdom on earth.[50] Micah's breathtaking tour of that history does not unfold in a straight line, though. Instead it moves back and forth from the distant future to the more recent, from events that are future even for us to events that are in our past. From a New Testament perspective, when Micah probes the question of the ruler of Israel in the future days, he gives some important teaching about the Messiah.

The Kingship to Be Restored (4:8)

Micah refers to the "watchtower of the flock" (4:8), which may be a poetic reference either to Jerusalem or possibly to the remnant of the people who are righteous by virtue of their faith in the Lord. There are many ancient watchtowers in Israel, constructed of stone and able to house a family temporarily. Normally these were built to protect vineyards from thieves and predators (see Isa. 5:2). A similar structure may have been used on occasion for protecting flocks (2 Chron. 26:10). The righteous remnant could have been like a watchtower in the sense that they kept the nation from complete destruction by their faithful obedience (compare Gen. 18:23–32; Isa. 10:20–22; Joel 2:32; Zeph. 3:9–13).

"Watchtower of the flock" actually has the same Hebrew words in it as the place name Migdal Eder (Gen. 35:21), evidently located between one and two miles east of Bethlehem.[51] For this reason, some think Micah is referring to Bethlehem, the birthplace of David.[52] The ancient Jewish translation of verse 8 (in the Aramaic language) even calls Migdal Eder "the anointed one [or, 'Messiah'] of Israel who was sheltered from the sins of the assembly of Zion." Words may mean one thing, but remind the hearer of something else. For example, "palm tree" may refer to a specific tree, but remind people of a tropical island. Something like this seems to be happening with what Micah is saying here. He means first of all a tower which has been constructed to protect a flock of sheep, that is, the people of Israel. The name surely reminds the listener, though, of Migdal Eder, that famous place near Bethlehem where Jacob pitched his tent. Bethlehem stirred up the additional thought that it was the birthplace of David, the ancestor of the Messiah. Later (5:2)

Micah will take up this very thought of the coming King who will be born in Bethlehem and rule over His people.

In addition, Micah mentions the "stronghold of the Daughter of Zion." The "stronghold" evidently refers to the highest part of the ancient City of David where it joins with the temple mount. It was the highest spot in the City of David (a part of Jerusalem) and the site of David's palace (2 Chron. 27:3; 33:14; Neh. 3:26–27; 11:21).[53] Once again Micah refers to the protection that this part of the city gave to the people.

The term "daughter" is often connected with cities in the Old Testament, particularly with either Zion or Jerusalem. Elaine Follis, who has studied this idiom, states that the expression "daughter of Zion" is more "than simply the personification of a group of people. Rather, it is an image of the unity between place and people within which divine favor and civilization create a setting of stability, of home, of fixedness."[54] It is this restoration of former stability and favor from the Lord which Micah evokes with his powerful imagery in 4:8.

Three short prophecies are included in this larger section about kingship.[55] First, Micah wonders about the pain and agony of the nation which will lose its king and go into exile to Babylon (4:9–10). Second, he reassures Israel that the plans of the nations cannot stand in the face of what the Lord has planned for His people (4:11–13). Finally, he prophesies the rise of a new ruler to be born in Bethlehem (5:1–6).

Israel Without a King (4:9–10)

When the leader of a country is suddenly assassinated or exiled, the people may feel extreme grief or a sense of abandonment. It sends a shock through the entire population that everyone shares in collectively. Such is the deep suffering that Micah foresees for his people, an agony that he compares to a woman in labor. Their king and counselor snatched away from them, the people leave their city for the miseries of Babylon.

In character with the rest of his prophecy, however, Micah holds out the hope of rescue. The Lord Himself will redeem His people from their situation in Babylon. Many have wondered about the time in history to which Micah's prophecy of exile in Babylon and ultimate restoration refers. From our perspective, we look back and see that in 586 B.C. Nebuchadnezzar of Babylon conquered Jerusalem and took the people into captivity (2 Kings 25; 2 Chron. 36:15–21; Jeremiah 52). We also see that in 538 B.C. Cyrus of Persia allowed the people of Judah to return to their land (2 Chron. 36:22–23; Ezra 1:1–4). This is the only historical fulfillment that fits exactly with what Micah says.

From Micah's perspective, these events were future; he speaks of "now" (4:9, 11) only to show the certainty and urgency of the Lord's word. No king of Judah in Micah's lifetime was either exiled or killed. Babylon was under Assyrian domination, but the powerful Merodach-Baladan of Babylon tried to assert his independence from Assyria (see 2 Kings 20:12; Isa. 39:1). Sennacherib, the king of Assyria, conquered much of Judah and threatened Jerusalem itself, but he was unable to succeed in this effort (2 Kings 18:17–19:37; 2 Chron. 32:1–23; Isaiah 36–37). Micah, like the prophet Isaiah, learned from the Lord that Babylon would ultimately be the greater threat to Jerusalem, but neither prophet knew how or when their prophecies would come to pass.

The Plans of the Lord Versus the Plans of the Nations (4:11–13)

Micah turns from rescue out of the Babylonian captivity to a time when Israel will defeat all of her enemies in battle, devoting the spoils of war to the Lord. It is difficult to find any time in Israel's history when this has taken place. Sennacherib had to return home after his defeat at the hands of the angel of the Lord, but Micah speaks of many nations and participation by the forces of Israel (called "daughter of Zion" because that was the capital and spiritual center of the nation). During the period of the Maccabees (first and second cent. B.C.) the Jews won some important battles against the Syrians; but again this does not seem to fit the language of "many nations," and the corruption of the religious leaders during this period does not fit with the devotion of the spoils to the Lord. Some of the victories of modern Israel have been against several nations at once, but it cannot be said that the Israelites have devoted the spoils of war to the Lord.

Charles Feinberg is probably correct to refer Micah's words to "the last great attack of the nations of the world against Israel,"[56] an event that is mentioned by other prophets as well (see Isa. 29:5–8; Ezekiel 38–39; Dan. 11:36–12:1; Joel 3:9–16; Obad. 17–21; Zech. 12:2–5; 14:1–5). At that time the nations of the world will attack Jerusalem and defeat the city at first, causing the people to flee. Then the Lord will empower His people with supernatural strength to defeat the enemy. According to the dispensational view, the time frame for this will be after the Rapture of the church (see 1 Thess. 4:15–17) and just prior to the return of Christ to set up the millennial kingdom.

The nations of the world do not consider the plans of the Lord (4:12). Their plan is to humiliate and embarrass the nation. However, the Lord's promise to Abraham is valid forever (Gen. 12:2–3; 22:15–18), and the nations cannot fight against the Lord Himself. The act of gathering sheaves to the threshing floor often serves in Scripture as a figure for judgment (Isa. 21:10; 27:12; 41:15; Jer. 51:33; Dan. 2:35; Matt. 3:12; Luke 3:17). Micah describes succinctly how Israel will actually defeat in battle the enemy nations. The Lord brings them to the "threshing floor" and then commands the "daughter of Zion" to "rise and thresh." The threshing of grain would sometimes involve oxen that would pull a sledge or cart, sometimes with sharp stones or pieces of metal attached to its underside, over the grain after it was spread out on the floor (Deut. 25:4). The iron horns and bronze hooves may have reference to the pieces of metal under the sledge (see also Amos 1:3). In any event, the "horn" symbolized strength or power (see 1 Sam. 2:1, 10; Jer. 48:25; Ezek. 34:21; Zech. 1:18–21).

The Rise of a New Ruler (5:1–6)

At the beginning of his prophecy about the king in Israel, Micah saw a vision of the people in great pain because they had no king (4:9). Micah now returns to this theme, predicting that enemy troops will defeat and dishonor Israel's ruler (5:1). That need not discourage the people, however, for the Lord plans to raise up a new ruler who will be born in Bethlehem, the birthplace of David (5:2). Until he is born the nation will be "abandoned" or given over to occupation by enemy powers (5:3). After his birth the divided nation will be reunited, and the new ruler will establish the kingdom of peace (5:4–5a) that Micah described in 4:1–5. At that time no nation ("Assyria") will be able to stand against Israel in her land; the new ruler will deliver his people from every threat (5:5b–6).

The Lord did not reveal to Micah just when or how these things would occur, but from the vantage point of later history it is possible to supply some details. The king who was struck on the cheek with a rod was evidently Zedekiah, the last king of Judah (see 2 Kings 25:1–7).[57] The period of abandonment would then be from the fall of Jerusalem in 586 B.C. to the birth of Jesus Christ (5:3a). It would also include the age of the church, because the twelve tribes of Israel have not yet been reunited in their land (5:3b). Micah foresaw the birth of Christ and His earthly reign, but he was not shown the long period of time between those two events. In other words, Micah 5:4–6 will not be fulfilled until the second coming of Christ.

All of these events had meaning for Micah and his generation. As far as he knew, everything could have happened in his lifetime. The fact that it did not does not lessen the significance of Micah's faith or of the faith of others in his time who chose to believe his message. They became part of that great company through the ages that has chosen to look for "the city with foundations, whose architect and builder is God" (Heb. 11:10).

The "city of troops" (5:1) refers to Jerusalem, and it may mean either that Jerusalem was protected by her own troops or that the enemy troops were surrounding the city. The "ruler" who is struck is literally the "judge" (as in Amos 2:3), even as the Lord in the last days will judge His people (Mic. 4:3). Micah uses a variety of terms for Israel's ruler in 4:8–5:6, including "king" (4:9), "counselor" (4:9; see also Isa. 9:6), "judge" (5:1, NASB; see also 2 Kings 8:1–6; Isa. 11:3–4; 16:5), and "ruler" (5:2, a different term in the Heb. than is found in the NIV of 5:1).

Micah develops two important facts about the coming ruler in 5:2. First, his arrival will be due entirely to the work of the Lord. This is not a human plan, but a divine drama that will reveal the sovereign power of Israel's God. Second, the coming one will be from the line of David, in accordance with the Lord's plan to establish David's kingdom forever (2 Sam. 7:16). Micah and the other writing prophets carefully weave together these two issues. It will not be the might and skill of humans, but the Lord, by His power and deliberate plan, will elevate a future descendant of David's line to be king over all the earth.

Ephrathah may have been the name of a clan that was a part of the tribe of Judah (Ruth 1:2; 4:11; 1 Sam. 17:12), or it may have referred to the district where Bethlehem was located.[58] Bethlehem was evidently the main town in Ephrathah's small territory, and the two became associated in order to distinguish the place from another Bethlehem in the north. Bethlehem would have seemed insignificant in comparison to Jerusalem or Lachish or some other large city in Judah or Israel; it is not even included among the list of cities that were settled after the first group of Judeans returned to their land from the Babylonian captivity (Neh. 11:25–31).[59] This is one of many instances in Scripture where the Lord uses something that seems insignificant in human eyes to reveal His divine power and wisdom (see Zech. 4:6; 1 Cor. 1:18–25).

God also says that this ruler will come "for me." In other words, he will arrive according to the Lord's plan and will carry out that plan. When the Lord sent Samuel to select David from among Jesse's sons to be king over Israel, He instructed the prophet to anoint "for me the one I indicate" (1 Sam. 16:3). Perhaps Micah wants his readers to reflect on this earlier conversation.[60]

Bethlehem was also David's hometown (1 Sam. 16:4–13), and the second main point of the passage is that this coming ruler will be in David's line. This is also stressed by the statement that the Messiah's "origins are from of old, from ancient times." The King James translators made it sound like the verse primarily relates to the eternal preexistence of the Messiah: "whose goings forth have been from of old, from everlasting" (see also the NASB). The NIV is more accurate here with "origins" and "ancient times." The term translated "everlasting" in the KJV often has that sense, but it means "ancient times" or "days of old" when it is paired with another word which is literally "day" (Deut. 32:7; Isa. 63:9, 11; Amos 9:11; Mic. 7:14; Mal. 3:4).[61] The other term, "goings forth" or "origins," can be applied easily to a genealogical origin in that various generations "go out" or proceed from the parents. The prophecy most likely refers to the Messiah's origins or descent from David. That is the whole point for mentioning Bethlehem, the birthplace of David himself. As Waltke expresses the significance of Micah's statement for the context, "Messiah is no upstart or afterthought in God's program. His origins began when God chose David in the first place."[62]

The view that Micah 5:2 refers to the preexistence of the Messiah from eternity has been a traditional interpretation from at least the time of the Latin Vulgate (fifth century), and it has modern supporters.[63] C. F. Keil, in his classic work on the Minor Prophets, tries to show that the verse teaches both the Davidic lineage of the Messiah and His preexistence.[64] The Messiah's preexistence is in any case a natural conclusion from His identification with God Himself (see Ps. 110:1; Isa. 9:6; Zech. 12:10); and while Micah 5:2 does not yield that teaching easily, it is consistent with it.

The woman who gives birth (5:3a) most probably is to be identified with the mother of the Messiah. Micah has already called Israel without a king "like" a woman "in labor" (4:9), but here he distinguishes between Israel and the woman and has just talked about the birth of the Messiah in Bethlehem. The nation continues to be abandoned until "the rest of his brothers return to join the Israelites" (5:3b). The Lord has not yet fulfilled His promise to reunite the divided tribes of Israel, so the Messiah still has not come to rule as king over the earth. However, His birth set in process events that marked the start of a new work of God in the world. Now is the time when "everyone who calls on the name of the Lord will be saved" (Joel 2:32; Acts 2:21), and that gives new hope to both Jew and Gentile (see Acts 2:38–39).

Even though Micah 5:4–6 will be fulfilled at the second coming of Christ, the verses still have a spiritual application to the present age of grace. Christ is currently shepherding the flock of those who have chosen to believe in Him (John 10:11, 14; Heb. 13:20; 1 Peter 2:25; 5:4), and He does so "in the strength" and "in the majesty of the name of the Lord" (see Heb. 1:3–4; 2 Peter 1:16). He provides His flock with inner security and peace, no matter how stressful or chaotic the outward circumstances might be (see John 14:27; 16:33; Eph. 6:15; Phil. 4:7; Col. 3:15).

The second part of verse 5, which mentions Assyria, seems at first glance to shift abruptly the topic back to Micah's own day. In fact, the Lord did save Jerusalem from the Assyrian king Sennacherib, possibly shortly after Micah gave this prophecy. Two clues show that Micah is still discussing the time of the millennial kingdom. First, the end of verse 6 says that the Messiah ("he") will deliver the nation from Assyria. Second, Micah mentions "the land of Nimrod" in addition to Assyria, a designation which means that the prophet has something broader than just Assyria in mind. Nimrod is mentioned only three other places in the Bible (Gen. 10:8–9; 1 Chron. 1:10), and in Genesis he is viewed as the founder of both Babylonia and Assyria (Gen. 10:8–12).[65] Micah apparently viewed Assyria, the major world power of his day, as symbolic of all the kingdoms of the world (see Zech. 10:11). It was "the land of Nimrod," the "mighty hunter" who founded both the nations that eventually were responsible for the downfall of Israel and Judah.[66] Isaiah and Micah both predicted that, in the future, Assyria and Egypt will worship the Lord together with Israel (Isa. 19:23–25; Mic. 7:12), another indication that the nation of Assyria is representative of many nations of the world, all of which will worship the Lord in the messianic times. It may be, as well, that the defeat of Sennacherib by the angel of the Lord in 701 B.C. informs Micah's statement. He would be saying, in effect, "Sennacherib could not take Jerusalem, and we will conquer and rule any future 'Assyria' which invades our land."

Micah's audience probably did not think of the numbers seven and eight ("seven shepherds" and "eight leaders of men" who "will rule the land of Assyria" and "the land of Nimrod"; 5:5–6) as literal figures. The sequence of numbers of the pattern x . . . x+1 is a literary device used often by poets throughout the ancient Near East to indicate progression toward a climax. Numerical sequences are found, for example, in the first two chapters of Amos and in Proverbs 30.[67] The number seven is commonly thought to signify perfection or totality, and Micah's point may be that Mesopotamia, the source of Israel's ancient enemies, will come under their rule in the coming kingdom. Such a reversal of the situation in Micah's day will all be possible because the Messiah "will deliver us from the Assyrian."

The military imagery of verse 6 seems surprising, especially in light of the security and peace spoken of in verses 4 and 5. Micah predicts a pattern that is known from other prophets, though (Amos 9:12; Obad. 18–21; Zech. 14:1–5). The Lord will give His people supernatural power to defeat all their enemies; then He will bring peace to the world, but only through a severe rule in which He crushes all rebellion immediately (see Ps. 2:9; Rev. 12:5). During that time, the Lord will delegate ruling the nations to His people (Dan. 7:27; Rev. 2:26; 20:4; compare Luke 19:11–27).

For all who live on this side of the birth in Bethlehem, Micah's words reveal the faithfulness and mercy of the Lord even more than they did for the Israelites in the seventh century B.C. We have the advantage of observing the wonderful fulfillment of this prophecy in the birth of Jesus Christ, whose line of descent goes back not only to David but also to His eternal relationship within the Trinity as the Son of God. Now is the time when anyone can trust the Good Shepherd to lead the way to secure paths and to give all the spiritual strength and nourishment needed to overcome the influence of the Evil One.

Lifting Up the Remnant to Triumph Over Its Enemies (5:7–9)

To this point Micah has preached about three major parts of the future kingdom: the Law of the Lord going out to the world from Jerusalem (4:1–5); the people who were exiled restored to their land (4:6–7); and the Messiah established as the new ruler or king (4:8–5:6). Now he deals with two issues concerning how the judgment that will come soon and the restoration in the more distant future are both tied together in the Lord's plan. First, the Lord reassures the people that it is His will for Israel to remain as a people. A remnant will not only survive, but they will also triumph over their enemies. Second, the Lord underlines the purpose of the judgment: It is to destroy everything in the land which the people have turned to for security instead of their God.

What does Micah mean by "the remnant of Jacob" (5:7)? In a strictly physical sense it would be all the people of Israel who survive all the years of exile from their land and who are alive at the time when the Lord establishes His kingdom on earth. The context indicates a spiritual sense too. As the apostle Paul said, "Not all who are descended from Israel are Israel," and it is "the children of the promise who are regarded as Abraham's offspring" (Rom. 9:6, 8). So also the Old Testament prophets thought of a righteous remnant that would emerge from the fiery judgments of the Lord, because the wicked will be destroyed in their sins (see Isa. 10:20–22; Amos 9:9–11; Zeph. 3:13). From another perspective, the Lord Himself will make the remnant righteous when He pours out His Holy Spirit upon them (see Isa. 44:3; 59:21; Ezek. 36:27; 37:14; 39:29; Joel 2:28–29; Zech. 12:10).

Micah must have something of the spiritual condition of the people in view when he uses the similes of "dew" and "showers." God is the source of these natural phenomena, and Micah's point is that what he is about to describe is entirely a work of the Lord. The morning dew and the showers of rain "do not wait for man or linger for mankind." That is, humans have no control over when they come.

Some think that Micah refers to the benefit that the moisture gives to the grass and the soil as well as to its heavenly origin,[68] while others think that the harsh imagery of an attacking lion in the next verse is incompatible with a beneficial effect.[69] Both concepts are possible if the response of the nations is taken into consideration; the remnant will bring refreshment to those among the nations who will trust the Lord but defeat for those who rebel against Him. The Lord promised Jacob, like Abraham, that "all peoples on earth will be blessed through you and your offspring" (Gen. 28:14). A similar concept is implied already in Micah 4:2, where the nations that desire to seek the Lord must have learned of Him through His people. Israel will triumph over her foes shortly before the kingdom will be set up, and it may be that the ministry of refreshment refers to the same period (compare 2 Cor. 2:14–16). In another sense, that ministry has already occurred with the coming of Jesus Christ through the Jewish people and the spread of the gospel to all parts of the ancient world through His apostles and the early believers (see Acts 8:4).

Lions were common in Israel in Old Testament times and a danger to both animals and people (1 Sam. 17:34; 2 Sam. 23:20; 1 Kings 13:24; 20:36; 2 Kings 17:25). No one will be able to "rescue" the nations from Israel, though the Lord will "deliver" Israel from the Assyrian (5:6). The same Hebrew word lies behind both "rescue" and "deliver" in these verses, and Micah apparently intends his listeners or readers to make the connection. When the Lord does something on behalf of His people, it always succeeds.

From the context it appears that verse 9 applies to the "remnant of Jacob" mentioned in verse 7, though it might possibly be addressed to the Lord. Because of the supernatural strength the Lord will give to His people, they will triumph over all their enemies.

Everything Contrary to the Lord Destroyed from the Land (5:10–15)

Throughout Israel's history the people were tempted to trust in something other than the Lord. Moses and the prophets warned them not to trust in the military strength of horses and chariots (Deut. 17:16; 20:1; 2 Kings 6:15–17; Ps. 20:7; Isa. 31:1); nevertheless, the kings of Israel came to depend on them (1 Kings 4:26; 2 Chron. 1:17; 9:25). Once the Lord has destroyed the horses and chariots, the people will no longer rely on them.

In addition, the people trusted in their walled cities and fortresses ("strongholds"). Because Jerusalem was spared the wrath of Sennacherib of Assyria, some even began to think that the city with Solomon's temple in it could not fall (Jer. 7:1–15; 26:1–6). These false sources of trust too must be pulled down.

The period of Micah was characterized as well by efforts to control life through the forbidden practices (Deut. 18:9–12) of magic spells and witchcraft (see also Isa. 2:6; 47:9, 12). These practices were associated with foreign influences and were often associated with idolatry that also came into Israel through assimilation with Canaanite religion (see 2 Kings 9:22; 2 Chron. 33:2–6; Isa. 2:6; Nah. 3:4). The Lord announces His plan to destroy all forms of illegitimate practices through which the people were trying to gain their own ends.

In addition to destroying every external hope of the Israelites, the Lord vows to "take vengeance in anger and wrath" upon disobedient nations. In this context the Lord's statement underscores the gravity of Israel's disobedience. She is no better than any pagan nation when she adopts their offensive practices. Another emphasis may be that Israel will no longer be able to rely upon her alliances with other nations. The Lord in His sovereignty will destroy all the nations that are disobedient to His requirements, including Israel and her allies.

All of this destruction may seem harsh or severe, but its purpose must be kept in view. The Lord promised that a remnant would survive not only from Israel, but also from the nations. When the Lord removes all sources of help, the only thing left is to call upon His name for salvation. Many are doing that even now during the special age of God's grace through His Son, Jesus Christ, but it will happen in an even more spectacular way in the new age yet to come.

14

THE LORD'S COMPLAINT AGAINST HIS PEOPLE

MICAH 6:1–16

When someone shows love to another person, either by words or by an act of kindness, it is surprising when the recipient rejects or ignores what has been said or done. We would consider that person ungrateful. Yet that is the way that the people of ancient Israel treated God. Actually, the case of Israel's rejection of God's love can be taken further. One of the most fundamental truths of the human condition is that ever since Adam and Eve the relationship between God and humanity has been wounded deeply, even to the point of complete separation. Scripture's consistent message, though, is that God does not want it to be that way; He longs to restore the relationship with those who have been created in His own image.

Common human experiences were used frequently by the prophets to help the people understand deep theological truths. For example, Hosea, by his own marriage, portrayed the Lord as a rejected lover (Hosea 1–3), and Isaiah composed the "Song of the Vineyard" to convey the great pain that God feels when His people spurn His efforts to take care of them (Isa. 5:1–7). Micah deals with the same topic by picturing a confrontation that he mediates between the people of Israel and the Lord. Some scholars have thought that it may even take the form of a challenge in court, with the Lord presenting His case against the people before the mountains.[70]

THE CASE AGAINST THE PEOPLE (6:1–12)

Micah calls on the Lord at first to present His case before an enduring monument to His faithfulness, the mountains and hills of the land of Israel itself (6:1–2). Then the Lord, speaking through the prophet, reminds the people of His own acts of love when He brought them into the land after He delivered them from slavery in Egypt (6:3–5). The people respond with a question (6:6–7): "With what shall I come before the Lord?" In other words, what will it take to please the Lord? The answer seems surprising; we might have thought Micah would say, "Bring whatever sacrifice the Law of Moses requires." Instead, he replies that the Lord wants His people to serve Him with a humble heart, not to bribe Him with gifts to win His approval of their wicked ways (6:8). Perhaps the people thought they could do the Lord a favor by bringing an offering, or perhaps they hoped to earn something from Him in return, even as they tried to get what they wanted from their idols or from their sorcerers. Finally, the Lord reminds the people that their sins of injustice give the lie to their seemingly pious desire to please Him (6:9–12). The second part of chapter 6 (vv. 13–16) predicts punishment for the people with such a perverted religion.

God's Complaint Witnessed by the Mountains and Hills (6:1–2)

From the English translation of 6:1 it might seem that those whom Micah calls on to hear the Lord's word are the same ones that are asked to plead their case before the mountains. However, the original Hebrew has two different ways to speak to someone, depending on whether only one or more than one person is being addressed.[71] When Micah says "listen" (6:1) he is talking to more than one, but when he says "stand up, plead your case," he is talking to only one person. It would have been possible to address the nation of Israel as a unit with the usage for one person, but the contrast of the two forms here makes it more likely that he calls upon the people to "listen" to what he has to say (compare 1:2; 3:1, 9; 6:9) and invites the Lord to "plead" his case.[72] In other words, the connection between the two parts of verse 1 is rather loose, with the first part referring to the new section of the prophecy. Another reason for this view is that Micah says the case or complaint is the Lord's, not Israel's (6:2). Once the Lord begins to speak directly in the proceedings (6:3), He calls for Israel to bring forward her issues, but it seems out of place for Israel to have the first word. The NIV represents this perspective by setting off 6:1a as a title and by using quotation marks to show that all of 6:1b–2 are the words of Micah.

The significance of the mountains and hills probably has to do with the ancient custom of setting up stones as a reminder of an agreement between two parties.[73] For example, Jacob set up stones in Gilead as a "witness" between himself and Laban that neither one would cross with hostile intent the boundary that it marked (Gen. 31:45–53). More to the point, Joshua led the people of Israel in a ceremony to renew the covenant with the Lord, with half of them standing in front of Mount Gerizim and half in front of Mount Ebal. Then he read "all the words of the law —the blessings and the curses—just as it is written in the Book of the Law" (Josh. 8:30–34). After the conquest of the land, Joshua led the people in another ceremony at Shechem (which lay between Mount Gerizim and Mount Ebal) and erected "a large stone . . . under the oak near the holy place of the Lord" (Josh. 24:26). "This stone will be a witness against us," Joshua said, because "it has heard all the words the Lord has said to us. It will be a witness against you if you are untrue to your God" (24:27). The Lord created the mountains, and they stood as an enduring reminder that He always remains faithful. They were excellent representatives to hear the charges brought against Israel.

As he so often does, Feinberg captures the broader implications of what is about to take place in Micah's drama: "What should strike us most in this is God's amazing condescension in thus reasoning with His creatures."[74] That he chose to do so was a sign of His grace and everlasting love, even for the people who had rejected Him.

God's Complaint in Light of His Past Treatment of Israel (6:3–5)

When the Lord tells His side of the dispute, He reminds the

people of how He has expressed His love for them in the past, bringing them out of their slavery in Egypt and guiding them through the wilderness to the Promised Land. In light of such a powerful display of His grace and mercy, He expresses surprise that they have turned away from Him. Like a wounded lover, He asks, "What have I done to you?" The hostility of humankind against God runs very deep in that even God's most miraculous displays of love are soon forgotten, and idols so quickly take His place. As Paul put it, "They exchanged the truth of God for a lie, and worshiped and served created things rather than the Creator" (Rom. 1:25).

The events that encompassed the exodus from Egypt to the entrance into Canaan became the defining act of God's salvation in the Old Testament, even as the events from the cross to the resurrection and ascension of Christ defined His salvation in the New Testament. A majority of the writing prophets mention some part of the Exodus events (see Isa. 63:11–14; Jer. 11:3–5; Ezek. 20:4–12; Dan. 9:15; Hos. 2:14–15; Amos 2:10; Hab. 3:8–15; Hag. 2:5; Mal. 4:4).

Micah lists five positive aspects of that period. First, the people were delivered from a foreign country. They would not be a nation if the Lord had not loved them. Second, they were delivered from slavery. Third, He provided outstanding leaders for them. Moses and Aaron stood up to Pharaoh on their behalf (Ex. 7–11). Later Moses gave them the Law (Ex. 19), and Aaron became the first high priest (Ex. 28:1). Miriam was a prophetess who led the people in a victory celebration after the passage through the Red Sea (Ex. 15:19–21).[75] How different these notables were from the leaders of Judah in Micah's day who were taking the people away from the Lord (chaps. 2–3). Fourth, the Lord frustrated the evil plans of Balak and Balaam (Numbers 22–24; 31:16).[76] Should the people now consider Him powerless against superpowers such as Assyria, Babylon, or Egypt? Fifth, the Lord led them into the Promised Land itself, moving them across the Jordan River from Shittim, their last encampment east of the Jordan (Josh. 3:1), to Gilgal, their base of operations within Canaan during the conquest (Josh. 4:19). The Lord's salvation was complete; He provided everything they needed right up to their first camping place in the land.

God's Complaint Demonstrated by Their Religious Practices (6:6–7)

After Micah invited the Lord to state His case against Israel before the ancient mountains, the Lord demanded that Israel make known any way in which He might have "burdened" the people. At the same time, He referred to His actions by which He literally brought the nation into existence and redeemed it from slavery. At last it is Israel's turn to respond, and their words betray the bankruptcy of their spiritual condition. They somehow have the mistaken impression that God's favor can be bought if only they can come up with the right price. They failed to see that the Lord wanted the worshipers' hearts, their whole being (Deut. 6:4–5); for this no sacrifice can substitute.

It might appear from a casual reading of 6:6–7 that Micah contradicts the Law of Moses. The burnt offering was the first of the offerings described in the book of Leviticus (chap. 1), and if it is sacrificed appropriately with a proper animal from the herd or the flock, "it will be accepted on his behalf to make atonement for him" (Lev. 1:4). If so, then why does Micah's rhetorical question seem to imply that burnt offerings have no value to make the worshiper acceptable to God? Virtually all interpreters agree that Micah was not denying the validity of the sacrificial system, but speaking out against a misunderstanding or misuse of that system.

We would not expect one part of Scripture to contradict another part, but there are other reasons as well for holding to the unity of the Old Testament on the subject of sacrifice. One reason is that in the list of offerings that Micah gives, the last one, child sacrifice, was actually condemned by the Law of Moses (Lev. 18:21; 20:2–5; Deut. 12:31).

A second reason is that, as Waltke notes, the Law of Moses also taught that "sacrifices without a spiritual commitment that displays itself in ethics profit nothing." This is seen by the fact that the Lord and His people ratified the covenant (Exodus 24) before the giving of the laws for sacrifice (Exodus 25–40). Also, when the people worshiped the golden calf (Ex. 32:1–6), "only after forgiveness for the breach of the prior covenant had been secured, did God resume instructions regarding worship."[77]

A third reason why Micah refers to an attitude that sacrifices could somehow bribe the Lord can be seen in the way the value of the offering gradually increases. After the "burnt offerings" and "calves a year old," with the amount unspecified, the worshiper wonders about "thousands of rams" or "ten thousand rivers of oil." King Solomon once offered a thousand burnt offerings on the altar at the high place in Gibeon, prompting the Lord to appear to him in a dream (1 Kings 3:4–5). So "thousands of rams" would be a price worthy of kings. Olive oil was used either in certain types of grain offerings or sometimes poured out or sprinkled before the Lord (see Gen. 28:18; Lev. 2:1–7; 14:10, 15–16). How much oil is in a "river" of oil, let alone in "ten thousand rivers of oil"? Obviously such an offering would be priceless, yet the worshiper takes the question one step further: "What about offering my own child?" This immediately reminds us of God's demand of Abraham that he sacrifice Isaac (Gen. 22:1–19); but there was also Ahaz, one of the kings of Judah during Micah's ministry, who "sacrificed his son in the fire" (2 Kings 16:3; cf. 17:17). Abraham's action was cut short once he demonstrated his faith in God, but Ahaz was "following the detestable ways of the nations the Lord had driven out before the Israelites" (2 Kings 16:3). Perhaps Micah even had Ahaz in mind as an example of what he was talking about. No matter what the cost of the sacrifice, it cannot buy acceptance with God. Ultimately it would be God's sacrifice of His own Son that would provide atonement for all who will accept it, placing their trust completely in what God has done.

Fourth, when the Lord brought a complaint about sacrifices against the people of Israel through Isaiah (Isa. 1:11–13), He even went so far as to condemn their prayers: "When you spread out your hands in prayer, I will hide my eyes from you; even if you offer many prayers, I will not listen" (Isa. 1:15). The reason is plain; it is because "your hands are full of blood". The Lord cannot accept the sacrifices of the people when they continue to oppress others unjustly.

An analogy can be made with the present day. Some might think that the Lord is pleased when they go to church regularly or put something in the collection plate. A prophet like Micah would tell them that such activities do nothing to gain favor with God if the worshipers do not live in a manner that pleases Him during the week (compare Rev. 3:15–20). This does not depreciate the value of attending church or giving an offering. It all depends on the heart of the worshiper, which must be right with God.

God's Complaint in Light of What He Really Desires (6:8)

Micah 5:2 and 6:8 are rightly the two most widely known verses of the book. The first tells of the One who will come to make people righteous, and the second gives God's definition of "righteous." Leslie Allen calls Micah 6:8 a "traditional answer" to the question of what God really requires.[78] This rings true when we examine the answer to this question given by various personalities of the Old Testament prior to and including the time of Micah.

Abraham illustrates well someone who walked humbly with his God, and he "believed the Lord, and he credited it to him as righteousness" (Gen. 15:6). Moses spoke of the need to love the Lord God with one's entire being (Deut. 6:5), as well as to love one's neighbor (Lev. 19:18). Some years later the prophet Samuel boldly told Saul that "to obey is better than sacrifice, and to heed is better than the fat of rams" (1 Sam. 15:22). Amos, who probably preceded Micah as a prophet, announced: "But let justice roll on like a river, righteousness like a never-failing stream!" (Amos 5:24) Could Micah possibly have had in mind Amos's river of justice as a counterpart to the "ten thousand rivers of oil"? Then there is the invitation from the Lord given by Isaiah, the contemporary of Micah: "'Come now, let us reason together,' says the Lord" (Isa. 1:18). Micah is providing a forum for just such a session of reasoning. All of these scriptural statements are getting at the answer to a question that is of great importance to every person: "How can I restore my broken relationship with the Almighty God?" In each case, though, the biblical writer highlights a slightly different facet of such a simple yet profound doctrine. Even so, it will be rewarding to examine in detail Micah's traditional yet uniquely beautiful formulation of God's heartfelt desire.

The introduction to the passage stands out. Micah seems almost surprised that the people are not already aware of the answer: "He has showed you, O man, what is good." In one sense, this is Micah's way of stressing that the answer he is about to give is traditional, but there is more to it than that. His use of the word "man" is unusual here; we might have expected "people" or "Israel." In addition, the Hebrew term for "man" is the same as "Adam," the first man. That term, however, refers to Adam only in Genesis 1–5 and a few other places (1 Chron. 1:1; Job 31:33, NASB; Hos. 6:7).[79] All the other times it is used, the word means "humankind" or people in general or an individual person, whether man or woman. Micah apparently wants to include, then, any and every person, not Israelites only. In this way he stresses not only what had been revealed in the Bible up to his time but also God's general revelation of Himself to humankind through creation and conscience (see Rom. 1:20; 2:14–15). That would make it all the more surprising that the Israelites could have thought that bringing sacrifices constituted the essence of a proper religion.

Micah's answer to the question consists of three simple phrases with only a few words: "to act justly and to love mercy and to walk humbly with your God." This statement breaks down further into two parts: a person's relationship with other people and his or her relationship with God. These are commonly referred to as "horizontal" relationships and the "vertical" relationship, respectively. In another sense, the parts cannot be separated in this way, because each of the three elements assumes a heart that is wholly committed to the Lord.

The concept of "justice" begins with the Lord Himself. He has already appealed to the issue of fairness when He compared what He has done for the people in the Exodus event with their feeble complaints that the Lord has mistreated or burdened them. It just doesn't seem fair or right for them to do that. God planted that sense of fairness within every soul, and He made it known as well through the Law of Moses and through His prophets (Mic. 3:8; 4:2). Possibly even the term for "man" that was chosen emphasizes the great distance between God and humankind. God as the Creator expects all of His creatures to uphold His standards, and He has every right to do so. The creature cannot argue with the Creator about what is right or fair (compare Rom. 9:19–21).

Micah gives many specific examples of what constitutes an unjust action: covetousness and greed (2:1–2); seizure of property and personal possessions through illegal and violent means (2:2, 8–9; 3:1–3, 10); bribery and illegal fees (3:11); dishonest sales practices (6:10–11); and untruthfulness (2:6–7; 3:5; 6:12). The positive model for justice is either the Lord Himself or His representative: punishing those who do wrong (1:5–7, 13; 2:3–4; 3:4, 12; 5:10–15; 6:9–12); settling disputes in a fair manner (4:3); governing the land in a way that causes peace (4:3–4; 5:4–5); and telling the truth (3:8). To "act justly," then, is to be in such close communion with God that His standards become clear and to obey those standards because they are God's. Near the close of the book, Micah says confidently that the Lord "establishes my right" (7:9), using the same Hebrew words translated here "act justly."

A similar thing can be said about "to love mercy." Mercy originates with God; He has shown it first, and therefore He expects His creatures to practice it (compare 1 John 4:19; Matt. 18:23–35). God showed His mercy even in His response to Adam and Eve's disobedience in the garden when He promised an "offspring" of the woman who will have the ultimate victory over the serpent (Gen. 3:15) and when he used animal skins to clothe them (Gen. 3:21). The term Micah uses for mercy stresses the Lord's loyalty or faithfulness to His covenant; time after time He has forgiven the people in order to maintain the covenant (see Ex. 34:5–10; Num. 14:1–22; Ps. 86:15; compare with the comments on Joel 2:13). Near the end of his book, Micah says of God, "[You] delight to show mercy" (7:18).

It is worthwhile to notice how appropriately Micah pairs each action term with its corresponding quality. We are to act justly but to *love* mercy. Justice is a duty, but mercy is a choice based on love. A person can treat people with fairness but still fail to show mercy if there is no love. In fact, the term for mercy can also be translated as "love" or "unfailing love" (Ps. 25:6; 40:11; 51:1; 69:16; 103:4; Jer. 16:5; Hos. 2:19; Joel 2:13). Love expresses itself in actions of mercy and compassion.

Another component of Micah's term for mercy is faithfulness or loyalty, a natural correlate of love since true love is faithful or loyal (see 1 Cor. 13:7–8). When David's son Absalom entered Jerusalem after David fled, he found Hushai, David's friend, and asked him, "Is this the love you show your friend?" (2 Sam. 16:17). The NASB has "loyalty" instead of "love," and the context easily yields the sense of either concept. Hushai must not "love" David (or so Absalom thought) if he was not "loyal" enough to go with him.[80]

Micah emphasizes in the context of 6:8 that the true worshiper of the Lord will love to demonstrate kindness and forgiveness to other human beings. As one who has himself drunk deeply of God's mercy, he will want to share that mercy with all who are around. This is the concept that Jesus Christ taught in His words to the Pharisees when they questioned why He would spend time with "tax collectors and 'sinners'": "It is not the healthy who need a doctor, but the sick. But go and learn what this means: 'I desire mercy, not sacrifice' " (Matt. 9:12–13; cf. 12:7; James 1:27). He quoted Hosea 6:6, another passage that has a meaning close to that of Micah 6:8.

The third thing the person does who follows the Lord properly is "to walk humbly" with God. "To walk with God" is an extremely common idiom in the Old Testament, meaning to serve Him or to please Him with one's whole life. Enoch, who was taken up directly to heaven, "walked with God" (Gen. 5:22, 24), and Noah was exceptional in his generation because he "found favor in the eyes of the Lord" and "was a righteous man, blameless among the people of his time, and he walked with God" (Gen. 6:8–9). Idolatry was to "follow [lit. 'walk'] after other gods" (Jer. 7:6, 9), and certainly Micah has in mind that this person worships the one, true God and no other. He also means, though, that the person can experience the presence of God because he or she is rightly related to Him through faith and seeks to please Him in daily life, a thought exemplified well by Abraham (see Gen. 24:40; 48:15).

Micah adds to the standard idiom the rare Hebrew word that means "humbly." It does not occur anywhere else in the Old Testament, but the same root is found in Proverbs 11:2. "Pride," says Solomon, results in "disgrace," but "humility" leads to "wisdom." As Dawes puts it, "These modest people pay attention to God but the proud listen only to themselves."[81] That is, humility defines an attitude toward life that rests comfortably in what God says to do, not insisting that the individual must operate exclusively on the basis of self-interest. It is actually the reverse of the sin of Adam and Eve, who were enticed by the statement that they could be like God in the knowledge of good and evil. That is, they wanted to make their own choices about what was good and what was bad, independently of what God told them. They came to know good and evil, but their "freedom" turned into bondage to sin, and their horizontal relations with each other deteriorated into blame and conflict. The humble walk with God results instead in the freedom of forgiveness (Mic. 7:18) and justice and mercy among all people (Mic. 4:2–4).

God's Complaint Demonstrated By Their Injustice (6:9–12)

Micah returns to the Lord's complaint after his instruction about what really pleases God. The Lord tells Jerusalem ("the city") to prepare for judgment in light of their wicked ways (6:9). There is too much dishonesty and violence within it to acquit her of the charge of rebellion, and the people were evidently not interested in Micah's plea for them to walk humbly with the Lord.

Many in the city were wealthy, but they acquired their riches only at the expense of others. Sometimes they acquired it even through outright dishonesty or violence (see also Amos 8:5). The "ephah" was a measure for grain, and the "short ephah" would be a means whereby the merchant would give the purchaser less grain than he thought he was buying. The same end could be achieved by balance scales and weights that were adjusted in favor of the seller. Lying and deceit were also found among the prophets who predicted prosperity rather than the judgment that Micah foresaw (2:6–7; 3:5), so it is not surprising to find those defects among the wealthy as well. As if deceit and lying were not enough to hoard up wealth into their coffers, some of the rich even went so far as to seize what they wanted by violence (see also 2:8; 3:10; and Amos 3:10, which uses the word "violence" of "plunder" gained through force). All these crimes simply prove that the Lord will be just when He brings about the destruction of Jerusalem.

The Punishment for the People (6:13–16)

The Lord tells the people how He will punish them for their disobedience, mentioning hardships that go along with enemy invasion and exile. The connection is made by the term "therefore" and by the notation, "because of your sins" (6:13). The section is similar to previous parts of the book in which the Lord has announced His judgment (1:6–16; 2:3–5; 3:12; 5:10–15), but here the language follows more closely traditional patterns found in other prophets and especially in the curses for disobedience given through Moses (Deut. 28:30, 33, 38; see also Amos 5:11; Zeph. 1:13; Hag. 1:6).

It is unusual that the Lord says, "I have begun to destroy you" (6:13; compare Jonah 3:4). Why would He refer to the beginning of the judgment? Perhaps He is referring to the difficulties of the war between Judah and Aram allied with northern Israel, or possibly He might mean the devastation of Judah by Sennacherib (see the Introduction to Micah). The destruction and ruin of the land described in Isaiah 1 may refer also to Sennacherib's doings.

The more traditional translation of Micah 6:13 is, "So also I will make you sick, striking you down" (NASB). The difference between "have begun" and "make (you) sick" is very slight in the original Hebrew, involving only the vowels and not the consonants.[82] The traditional reading is much harder to explain, though it could refer to the severity of the punishment.

The punishments fit the crimes (6:14–15). Those who

enjoyed the benefits of prosperity—eating well, storing up a surplus for hard times, planting many crops, pampering themselves with oil and wine—will find themselves suddenly having to endure empty stomachs and empty barns, struggling to get even the essentials for preserving life. The enemy occupation will use up all the good things of the land.

The second line of 6:14 is difficult and has led to different translations in the modern versions. The King James seems almost unintelligible: "and thy casting down shall be in the midst of thee." The NASB's rendering is only slightly easier to understand: "And your vileness will be in your midst." The NRSV is quite similar to the NIV: "and there shall be a gnawing hunger within you." The most difficult Hebrew term is taken variously as "casting down," "vileness," "gnawing hunger," or "empty." Also, the term translated "in your midst" or "within you" can also mean "your stomach." The NIV fits the context well and makes an excellent parallel with "you will eat but not be satisfied." Each of the verses in this section consists of a line followed by one or more lines that give a further explanation of it, so it is likely that the second line of verse 14 should develop the sense of the first line.

In the last verse in the section (6:16), the Lord gives an additional charge against the people and reiterates how He is going to judge them. This time, though, He adds the element of "derision" and "scorn" that the nations will heap up on Israel.

Omri was one of the most important of the early kings of the northern kingdom of Israel (885–873 B.C.). As the commander of the army, he came to power through a violent struggle (1 Kings 16:15–27), but he was able to establish a dynasty which lasted for some fifty years. His most outstanding achievement was the founding of the city of Samaria, which became Israel's capital until it was conquered by the Assyrians. From archaeological evidence at Samaria, it is clear that Omri and his son Ahab must have had strong ties with the Phoenicians.[83] From the Bible this is also clear, because Ahab married Jezebel, a Phoenician princess, and also introduced many elements of Phoenician Baal worship into Israel (see Introduction; 1 Kings 16:32–33; 18:19). While the author of Kings says Omri "did evil in the eyes of the Lord and sinned more than all those before him" (1 Kings 16:25), the "statutes of Omri" that Micah mentions are otherwise unknown. Certainly the "practices of Ahab's house" and "their traditions" are clear from the account in Kings. Micah must have been referring to the religious deviations that these two kings introduced into the northern kingdom. Eventually these same practices found their way into the southern kingdom of Judah through King Ahaziah, whose mother was Omri's granddaughter, and the Lord expressed His strong displeasure (2 Kings 8:26–27). Micah gives the general sense that these infectious practices continued in Judah right up to his own day.

Micah speaks of the nation's "ruin" in verses 13 and 16, giving a sense of closure to this part of his prophecy. The devastation of verse 13, though, was developed in terms of the deprivation of the people. At verse 16 it is developed in terms of their shame before the nations. The complete destruction of the land will be cause for the nations to sneer at the people, a severe punishment for the Israelites who took great pride in their nation and capital city of Jerusalem (see Isa. 3:16; 5:15).

With chapter 6, Micah concludes the main part of his prophecies about the Lord's judgment and salvation. In chapter 7, he will speak from the standpoint of one who serves the Lord, yet has to live in the evil society that he has been describing. In this way he is able to give a personal response to all that the Lord has spoken to the people through him.

15

THE HOPE OF THE GODLY

MICAH 7:1–20

Micah changes the style of his prophecy in the last chapter. Up to this point he has spoken for the Lord to the people, mostly even framing his prophecies with the word "I" when he means the Lord rather than himself. Now Micah becomes more meditative and distances himself from the prophetic burden, expressing his faith in the Lord's rightness and goodness in all that he will do to the nation. In this contemplation, he represents the righteous remnant of the people, "voicing the confession of the godly."[84]

The prophet uses three reflective literary forms to bring his prophecy to a conclusion that is full of hope and trust. The chapter can be divided into three parts on the basis of these forms, and they include a soliloquy about the desperate condition of the country (7:1–7), a personification of Jerusalem as someone who looks forward to her eventual victory (7:8–13), and a prayer or psalm that calls on the Lord to restore the people and that praises Him for His compassion and mercy (7:14–20).

THE CIRCUMSTANCES THAT MIGHT CAUSE DESPAIR (7:1–7)

As Micah thinks about his society, he runs through a long

list of problems that would cause most people to despair. While he starts out his inner dialogue with an outburst about his misery, at its conclusion he makes a confident statement of faith: "But as for me, I watch in hope for the Lord" (7:7).

The Disappearance of the Godly from the Land (7:1–4a)

As Micah scans his nation looking for a godly person, he is greatly disappointed to find none (7:1–2a). When the farmer harvested his field, he was supposed to leave behind for the poor or the alien what was at the very edges of the field or anything that was dropped on the ground (Lev. 19:9–10). Micah thinks of a situation where the crops are so poor that the destitute gleaner finds nothing in the fields to eat (7:1). Just as the gleaner sees no fruit remaining, so Micah discovers that "the godly have been swept from the land; not one upright man remains" (7:2a). Instead, all he can see is the terrible corruption described in the next few verses (7:2b–4a).

Violence was so prevalent that people would hunt down and even kill each other ("brother"; 7:2b). The rugged terrain of the Judean hills and mountains would make it easy to set an ambush, but Micah might be speaking figuratively for all sorts of murder, including cases where people died because others stole their source of livelihood from them by clever tactics (see 2:1–2, 9; 3:2–3, 10).

The "hands" that "are skilled in doing evil" stand for illegal practices (7:3a). A crooked official would take a bribe with his hands, and those in power made sure to take advantage of whatever situation they could to enrich themselves. Bribes were clearly forbidden by the Law of Moses (Ex. 23:8; Deut. 16:19; 27:25), but Micah observed the practice of accepting gifts for favors at all levels of government (see also 3:11). Amos and Isaiah also knew of this corruption of justice (Isa. 1:23; 5:23; Amos 5:12).

The last line of 7:3 is difficult to translate. The NASB is noncommittal ("so they weave it together"), while the NRSV and the NIV offer a choice between either the perversion of justice or a conspiracy. In the final analysis there is little difference between the two, because the conspiracy would be for the purpose of perverting justice.

Micah takes a low view of his fellow people. Even the best and most upright of them are, in reality, as dangerous as a brier patch or a thorn hedge (compare Prov. 26:9; Ezek. 28:24). To approach them is to risk heavy losses, possibly even of one's own life.

The Judgment of God on the People (7:4b)

The second part of 7:4 has several challenges to its proper interpretation. First, what is "the day of your watchmen"? Second, the NIV has supplied the word "God" under the assumption that it is implied in the text. Is this justified? Third, what is meant by "their confusion"?

The "watchman" would stand guard on the city wall; it was his job to sound the alarm or to announce the arrival of dignitaries (2 Sam. 18:24; 2 Kings 9:17; Ps. 127:1; Isa. 52:8; 62:6). This function made a natural analogy for the prophet, appointed by the Lord to spread the news from the Lord, good or bad, to his people (Jer. 6:17; Ezek. 3:17; 33:7; Hos. 9:8). Most have taken "your watchmen," therefore, to mean "your prophets." This is made clear by the TEV: "their watchmen, the prophets."[85]

If the "watchmen" are prophets, then "the day of your visitation" (literal trans.) probably refers to a visit from God, who brings to His people either judgment or blessing when He "visits." Here judgment would be the fitting consequence for such a corrupt people. When the term "visit" has this negative sense, the NIV most often uses a form of "punish" in its translation (see Ex. 20:5; 34:7; Lev. 18:25; Num. 14:18; Deut. 5:9; Job 35:15; Ps. 89:32).

Finally, "the time of their confusion" would be the chaos that results when God arrives with His judgment (see Isa. 22:5; Joel 1:18). Since Micah sets the time frame as "now," the verse could be paraphrased as follows: "The time for God to punish you, as foretold by the prophets, is already here. As soon as He arrives with that punishment, all of you will be thrown into a panic." Possibly Micah refers to the panic in the city from the invasion that he described earlier in the book (1:6–16; 2:4; 3:12; 4:11).

The Breakdown of Relationships in Society (7:5–6)

The "confusion" of the people may have suggested the total breakdown of relationships that Micah describes in 7:5–6.[86] No one can be trusted; the closest bonds of friendship and family mean nothing. A man cannot talk freely even in the presence of his own wife. As Waltke points out, "The judgment fits the crime: the leaders broke covenant with the people; now the ship of state breaks apart in God's judgment. The leaders could not be trusted; now all are suspicious of each other."[87]

Jesus Christ used the phrasing of Micah 7:6 to describe the kind of hostility between people that his ministry would cause (Matt. 10:35; Luke 12:53). This is a case not of the fulfillment of prophecy, but of using the language of Scripture to make a point which seems appropriate. Micah thought of a social breakdown caused by the sin of the people, whereas Jesus had in mind the division that His words would cause between those who believed Him and those who rejected Him. Possibly one could think of an extension of Micah's message in the sense that when Christ came into the world, He brought judgment that disrupted the fabric of society.

The Confidence of One Who Trusts in the Lord (7:7)

Micah concludes his soliloquy with a strong statement of trust in what the Lord will do. He has not been able to find any redeeming qualities in his countrymen, yet he hopes not in people but in the Lord. When he changes his focus from earth to heaven, his whole outlook changes too. Now he expresses with conviction that "my God will hear me." In other words, he can step back from the situation and wait for the Lord to take action; he can rest in the assurance that the Lord will vindicate the righteous at just the right time.

The word "watch" is from the same root as the "watchmen" of 7:4. Part of the function of a prophet is to "watch" for the word of the Lord to the people, like Habakkuk who said, "I will stand at my watch and station myself on the ramparts" (Hab. 2:1). Even so Micah will watch for the Lord to act according to His word.

Also the prophet watches for the Lord "in hope." It is characteristic of the godly that they "hope" in the Lord, confident that He will deliver them from whatever the present circumstances might be. Job is a prime example. As he sought an audience with God so he could state his case before Him, he declared boldly: "Though he slay me, yet will I hope in him" (Job 13:15). The verb is also common in the Psalms for the individual who puts his trust in the Lord: "I wait for the Lord, my soul waits, and in his word I put my hope" (Ps. 130:5).

The City That Will Be Victorious (7:8–13)

After his own declaration of trust in the Lord, Micah envisions a woman who addresses another woman who is her enemy.[88] In her speech she gives a theological explanation for why her enemy has defeated her. Her foe may gloat now in the exultation of victory, but it will not be a permanent victory. It is only because the believer has sinned against the Lord that she has suffered. Because she continues to trust in the Lord, He will eventually reverse her fortunes.

Who are these two women? Micah's response to the speaker in verses 11–13 establishes that the first woman that must be Jerusalem (compare 4:9–10), for he says that her walls will be rebuilt and her boundaries extended. The contents of the woman's speech, though, also show that she represents the remnant of God's people who have been scattered over the earth (see Mic. 2:12; 4:6–7). There may not be any specific enemy in mind for the other woman; all we are told is that she is gloating over Jerusalem's misfortune and that someday she herself will also fall (see 4:11). This could be true of Edom (Obad. 12), Babylon (Isa. 13:19), or of any and all that have participated in some way in the defeat and humiliation of Israel.[89]

Jerusalem believes that the Lord will be her light even when she sits in darkness (7:8). Confident hope and trust in the Lord is like a light. Knowing that He has life's dark times under control and that He has plans to deliver the believer shines the light of understanding and points the way to victory over the darkness. Eventually, "He will bring me out into the light" (7:9) where His plans are evident to all. Joseph seems to have experienced something similar. After a series of personal calamities, during which he maintained his trust in the Lord, he came to a point where he could say to his brothers, "You intended to harm me, but God intended it for good to accomplish what is now being done, the saving of many lives" (Gen. 50:20). The light shone brighter and brighter in his life until all could see the power of the Lord.

Having heard Jerusalem's declaration of confidence, Micah brings an additional word of reassurance to her from the Lord (7:11–13). Her trust is not misplaced; the Lord will see that her former glory is restored and even extended (see Ezek. 48:30–35; Amos 9:11–12; Obad. 20; Zech. 14:10–11). Also the remnant of Israel ("people") in exile will return to her from around the world (7:12). In contrast, the rest of the world will come under judgment for their role in Israel's defeat (7:13; see also 4:13; 5:5–9). All these things will happen in the future millennial kingdom of which Micah spoke in 4:1–8.[90]

The God Who Makes Hope Possible (7:14–20)

At the conclusion of his book, Micah includes a psalm that sums up the hope that he has for Israel's future. As a prophet he was responsible to pray for the people (see Gen. 18:22–32; 20:7; 1 Sam. 12:19, 23; Isa. 37:1–4; Jer. 7:16; 42:20; Hab. 3:1), and here he requests the Lord to once again lead His people like a shepherd (7:14). Then he records the Lord's response to that prayer: "I will show them my wonders" (7:15). After that Micah predicts how the nations will react to the Lord in the new age when He will intervene with miracles on behalf of His people. Finally, Micah gives praise to the Lord for His forgiveness and mercy which He grants to His people because of His covenant with Jacob, Abraham, and other founding fathers of the nation. Thus the book ends on a positive note. Even though many sorrows and difficulties await Israel in the future, those need not overwhelm the one whose faith in the Lord remains steadfast. The God who must judge the sinful nation is also the God who delights to show mercy to His repentant people.

The Prophet Prays for Restoration (7:14)

The imagery of the Lord as shepherd has always had a strong appeal to His people. It implies a completeness of trust in the goodness of the shepherd and a serenity of life free from care or anxiety (see Psalm 23). The shepherd uses the staff to guide the flock to a good pasture, and Micah's prayer expresses an intense longing for the Lord to move the people from their present state to a new situation filled with fresh blessings. The people are called "the flock of your inheritance." This singles Israel out as the Lord's special possession which He has chosen (see Joel 3:2; compare Ps. 78:71; Isa. 19:25).

Commentators are divided about how to understand Micah's words about the flock "which lives by itself in a forest, in fertile pasturelands." A forest does not normally seem like a good place for sheep. Their pasture should be in more open fields, and many of the forests of ancient Israel harbored dangerous animals (Isa. 56:9; Jer. 5:6; Hos. 2:12; Amos 3:4). Also the thought of being isolated or alone could be taken in a negative way (see Lev. 13:46; Isa. 27:10; Lam. 1:1). James Mays takes the term for "forest" more in the sense of "scrub," interpreting that "the image reflects a historical situation in which the nation's territory is confined to the hill country with the good grazing and farming land in the possession of others."[91] In this view, the prophet describes the lowly condition of Israel which leads to his longing for the Lord to let the flock "feed in Bashan and Gilead as in days of old."

This view requires the interpreter to assume a rather complicated relationship between "in a forest" and "in fertile pasturelands." That is, Israel is restricted by the forest and longing for the fertile pasturelands of their neighbors. It also seems unusual that the hill country of Judah would be viewed as inadequate for the people; but more importantly, the implication of 7:15, that the Lord will accomplish something equal to a new exodus for His people, is too powerful for a simple expansion of territory.

For these reasons, it seems best to take the entire verse as "prophetic in its outlook," as Feinberg puts it. "God is to feed the flock of His heritage as they dwell alone in security and without harm in the forest in the midst of Carmel."[92] The term for "fertile pasturelands" can also be taken as "Carmel," a range of mountains that separate the broad plain of Megiddo from the coastal plain and hill country of Israel. Mount Carmel was famous for its luxurious and abundant growth (Song 7:6). Isaiah 32:15 may give an important clue about Micah's prayer. It says that when God's Spirit "is poured upon" Israel "from on high," then the desert will become a "fertile field," and the fertile field will seem "like a forest." The same word translated "fertile field" is taken as "fertile pasturelands" in Micah 7:14, so both verses have the same term closely associated with the word for "forest." Probably Micah uses "forest" here to mean something like lush growth of vegetation. As for the expression "by itself," it may also indicate intimacy between the flock and the shepherd, as well as a sense of security in being isolated from possible enemies (Num. 23:9; Deut. 33:28; Ps. 4:8).

Bashan was a fertile area famous for its oak trees (Isa. 2:13; Ezek. 27:6; Zech. 11:2) and well-fed cattle and flocks (Ps. 22:12; Ezek. 39:18; Amos 4:1). It was located to the east of the Sea of Gaililee and the Huleh Basin (north of the Sea of Galilee). The area is today known as the "Golan Heights." Gilead was east of the Jordan but south of Bashan and north of Moab, and it was also "suitable for livestock" (Num. 32:1). Micah prays for the day when Israel will reoccupy all its old territory (compare Obad. 19–20). Early in his ministry, Gilead had been annexed by Assyria (2 Kings 15:29), and sometime later the entire northern kingdom became a part of the empire (2 Kings 17).

The Lord Promises a New Deliverance (7:15)

The Lord's promise in regard to Micah's prayer is interjected into the psalm: "As in the days when you came out of Egypt,

I will show them my wonders." The Lord is planning a new work among His people through which He will display His power to deliver them in a way that will make everyone remember the exodus from Egypt.

Many interpreters have had trouble with this verse because it seems too abrupt to suddenly hear God speaking in the middle of Micah's psalm.[93] It fits a pattern, though, of statement followed by response that has already occurred in the chapter. After Jerusalem spoke of her faith in the Lord (7:8–10), Micah responded to her with a fresh guarantee from the Lord to restore her to her former greatness (7:11–13). A similar explanation can be given for 7:7, in which Micah responds to his depressing observations about so much trouble in the land with his own affirmation of faith.

The Nations React to the Lord's Miracles (7:16–17)

When the Lord brought Israel out of Egypt under Moses, the nations became very afraid when they heard of the power that He exercised against Egypt and other nations (Ex. 15:14–16; Num. 22:2–4; Josh. 2:8–11). In the same way, the kingdoms of the earth will shrink back in terror when the Lord comes to restore His people to their land. Seeing His power, they will realize their own ineffectiveness. These who in the past boasted of their defeat of God's people will be unable to say a word in defense of themselves. They will also be deafened by the Lord's thundering voice in the judgment. The image of "licking the dust" like a snake shows their submission to the Lord (Ps. 72:9; Isa. 49:23).

The People Trust in the Lord's Mercy (7:18–20)

Micah's concluding words are centered around the mercy of the Lord.[94] Unlike the so-called "gods" of all the other nations, Israel's God is merciful. Through the psalm Micah praises the Lord for this quality of mercy, dwelling on specific ways in which He demonstrates it. He then concludes by expressing his confidence to the Lord that despite their situation now, He will again show mercy to the people in response to His covenant with the founding fathers of the nation.

The imagery of these last few verses is common in the psalms. The psalmists often questioned the Lord, "Will you be angry forever?" (Pss. 79:5; 85:5; compare 6:3; 13:1; 74:1; 80:4; 89:46; 90:13). That seems to be the constant cry from the heart of those who are deeply troubled or even overwhelmed by their afflictions. They trust in the Lord's goodness, but they cannot help but wonder, "How long?" David meditated on the mercy of the Lord and concluded, "He will not always accuse, nor will he harbor his anger forever" (Ps. 103:9). Through the prophets Isaiah (57:16) and Jeremiah (3:12) the Lord affirmed this teaching by His personal promise: "I will not accuse forever, nor will I always be angry." It is enough for the believer to have this assurance: "How long? Not forever." Perhaps the trouble might last a lifetime, but it is made bearable by the promise that it is only temporal; in the age to come there will be relief. Such assurance is the essence of the faith that is "sure of what we hope for and certain of what we do not see" (Heb. 11:1).

Micah parallels the conclusions of Psalm 103 in several notable ways. Both David and Micah focus their attention on the Lord's mercy (which equals "love" in the NIV of Ps. 103:4, 8, 11, 17); both place a limit on His anger; and both give a concrete image for how the Lord will treat the sins that He forgives. David sees Israel's transgressions removed "as far as the east is from the west" (Ps. 103:12), while Micah sees that the Lord "will tread our sins underfoot and hurl all our iniquities into the depths of the sea" (7:19). Both writers stress the thoroughness and finality of the Lord's forgiveness through these vivid word pictures.

The Lord's mercy to His people is grounded in the way He has chosen or elected them to salvation. For Israel this meant those two defining moments when the Lord called Abraham to leave his country and his family and journey to a land "I will show you" (Gen. 12:1) and when He chose Jacob rather than Esau to transmit the blessings of the covenant through his twelve sons (Gen. 28:12–15). For the Christian it means the work of Jesus Christ in His crucifixion, burial, and resurrection

(1 Cor. 15:3–7), events that have made God's salvation possible for all the world. The two works, for Israel and for the Christian, are tied together, however, through the promise to Abraham as well as to Jacob that through them the entire world will be blessed (Gen. 22:18; 28:14). How wise and perfect are the Lord's ways and His mercies to His people!

NOTES

Joel

1. That is, "Yahweh is God." Most modern versions render the divine name "Lord" unless it is preceded by the Hebrew word that means "Lord." These modern versions are consistent with Jewish tradition (especially as seen in the Greek Septuagint) and New Testament practice. The translation "Jehovah" is less accurate than "Yahweh." See Kenneth L. Barker, "YHWH Sabaoth: *'The Lord Almighty,'*" in *The NIV: The Making of a Contemporary Translation* (Grand Rapids: Zondervan, 1986), 106–9.
2. Gleason L. Archer, *A Survey of Old Testament Introduction,* revised and expanded (Chicago: Moody, 1994), 339–41. Archer relies heavily on the fact that Joel does not mention a king and on the nations that he names in Joel 3.
3. Richard D. Patterson, "Joel," in *Expositor's Bible Commentary,* ed. Frank E. Gaebelein (Grand Rapids: Zondervan, 1985), 7:230–33.
4. David Allan Hubbard, *Joel and Amos,* Tyndale Old Testament Commentaries (Downers Grove, Ill.: InterVarsity, 1989), 25–27; Thomas J. Finley, *Joel, Amos, Obadiah,* Wycliffe Exegetical Commentary (Chicago: Moody, 1990), 8–9.
5. A minority view among those who accept the full inspiration and authority of Scripture. But see, in addition to the works cited above, Roland Kenneth Harrison, *Introduction to the Old Testament* (Grand Rapids: Eerdmans, 1969), 876–79; Robert B. Chisholm, Jr., "Joel," in *The Bible Knowledge Commentary: Old Testament,* ed. John F. Walvoord and Roy B. Zuck (Wheaton, Ill.: Victor, 1985), 1409–10.
6. Cf. S. R. Driver, *The Books of Joel and Amos,* Cambridge Bible for Schools and Colleges (Cambridge: Cambridge Univ. Press, 1907), 24–25.

7. See E. J. Young, *Introduction to the Old Testament* (Grand Rapids: Eerdmans, 1949), 256.
8. Compare with Leon J. Wood, *The Prophets of Israel* (Grand Rapids: Baker, 1979), 267; Patterson, "Joel," 231.
9. Mentioned in the apocryphal book of Sirach (or Ecclesiasticus) 49:10.
10. See Finley, *Joel, Amos, Obadiah,* 5–6, for more details.
11. See Otto Eissfeldt, *The Old Testament; An Introduction,* trans. Peter R. Ackroyd (New York: Harper & Row, 1972), 568–70.
12. John Calvin, *Joel, Amos, Obadiah,* vol. 2 of Commentaries on the Twelve Minor Prophets, trans. John Owen (Grand Rapids: Baker, 1981), xv.
13. For more detail about the implications of Joel 2:28–32 for today, see the discussion below.
14. There is dispute about whether these verses narrate the past or predict future events (compare the NASB and the NIV against the NRSV). See the discussion on 2:18–19 for arguments in favor of the narration view.
15. Douglas Stuart (*Hosea–Jonah,* Word Biblical Commentary 31 [Waco, Tex.: Word, 1987], 232–34) suggests that even in the first chapter the locusts stand for an invading army, either the Assyrians or the Babylonians.
16. Richard Patterson ("Joel," in *Expositor's Bible Commentary,* ed. Frank E. Gaebelein [Grand Rapids: Zondervan, 1985], 7:245) thinks of the Assyrians or the Babylonians.
17. For hyperbole as a characteristic Semitic style of expression, see G. B. Caird, *The Language and Imagery of the Bible* (Philadelphia: Westminster, 1980), 110. Jesus often used hyperbole in his teaching (see, for example, Matt. 5:29–30).
18. Compare Charles L. Feinberg: "Joel starts with the situation then existing in the land after the havoc of the locust plague and then goes on to picture the dreadful Day of Jehovah yet future, but imminent" (*Minor Prophets* [Chicago: Moody, 1976], 75).
19. In Hebrew poetry it is common for the second of two parallel lines to intensify or extend in some way the first line (see comments on v. 6b).
20. In ancient Hebrew culture the "engagement" period was considered to be as binding as marriage itself, though it would not have been considered proper for the couple to have relations before the actual wedding.
21. See Gordon J. Wenham, *The Book of Leviticus,* New International Commentary on the Old Testament (Grand Rapids: Eerdmans, 1979), 69–72.
22. Elias D. Mallon, "A Stylistic Analysis of Joel 1:10–12," *Catholic Biblical Quarterly* 45 (1983): 537–48.
23. Some translations of verse 10 refer to the ground as "mourning," but the translation "dried up," as in the NIV, is fully justified in light of the word's etymology and usage elsewhere.
24. "Shaddai" may be related to a root word meaning "to destroy" (see Ruth 1:20–21; Job 6:4; 15:25; 21:15, 20; 23:16; 27:2; 31:2; 37:23; Ps. 68:14; Isa. 13:6) or to a word that means "mountain." The rendering

"Almighty" goes back to the Greek translation of the book of Job. (See also R. Laird Harris et al., eds., *Theological Wordbook of the Old Testament* [Chicago: Moody, 1980], 2:907.)

25. According to others, Joel 2:1–11 depicts an actual invasion by a future foreign army. See Richard D. Patterson, "Joel," in *Expositor's Bible Commentary,* ed. Frank E. Gaebelein (Grand Rapids: Zondervan, 1985); and Robert B. Chisholm, Jr., "Joel," in *The Bible Knowledge Commentary: Old Testament,* ed. John F. Walvoord and Roy B. Zuck (Wheaton, Ill.: Victor, 1985).
26. For a more detailed description, see Kenneth L. Barker, "Zechariah," in *Expositor's Bible Commentary,* ed. Frank E. Gaebelein (Grand Rapids: Zondervan, 1985), 7:619–20.
27. See Driver, *The Books of Joel and Amos,* 87–91; and Walter K. Price, *The Prophet Joel and the Day of the Lord* (Chicago: Moody, 1976), 33.
28. Leslie C. Allen, *The Books of Joel, Obadiah, Jonah and Micah,* New International Commentary on the Old Testament (Grand Rapids: Eerdmans, 1976), 70.
29. Joel uses an effective pun on the word "face" in verse 6. One might say the "appearance" of the locusts makes the "appearance" of the people pale.
30. There was no completed wall between the fall of Jerusalem in 586 B.C. and Nehemiah's mission in 444 B.C. If Joel was written about 500 B.C., he could have viewed the locusts as scaling the remains of the walls.
31. See Driver, *The Books of Joel and Amos,* 87–91; Price, *The Prophet Joel and the Day of the Lord,* 33.
32. The NASB and the KJV imply that Joel 2:11 describes the Lord as "mighty" or "strong." The NIV, however, correctly applies the adjective to the locust swarm ("mighty are those who obey his command"). The adjective in question normally means "numerous" ("strength in numbers") and is never elsewhere used of the Lord, though it also refers in Joel 2:2 to the locusts.
33. For further discussion of the theological problem of God changing His mind, see *The New Scofield Reference Bible* on Zecheriah 8:14 and Harris et al., *Theological Wordbook of the Old Testament,* 2:571.
34. "Those nursing at the breast" could hardly participate in a meaningful way. The statement should be taken as a figure of speech to stress participation by the entire community.
35. The NRSV translates with the past tense.
36. Two exceptions occur in Isaiah 9:6 ("will be" and "will be called"). Other factors about the grammar in that passage account for the deviations from the norm.
37. See Walter C. Kaiser, Jr., *The Uses of the Old Testament in the New* (Chicago: Moody, 1985), 166.
38. Cited by Julius A. Bewer, "A Critical and Exegetical Commentary on Obadiah and Joel," in *A Critical and Exegetical Commentary on Micah, Zephaniah, Nahum, Habakkuk, Obadiah and Joel* (1911; reprint, Edinburgh: T & T Clark, 1974), 113.

39. Walter K. Price (*The Prophet Joel and the Day of the Lord* [Chicago: Moody, 1976], 61) cites a 1915 report in *National Geographic* by John D. Whiting. See also Allen, *The Books of Joel, Obadiah, Jonah and Micah,* 88.
40. See Robert B. Chisholm, Jr., "Wordplay in the Eighth–Century Prophets," *Bibliotheca Sacra* 144 (1987): 52.
41. Patterson, "Joel," 7:254.
42. Kaiser (*The Uses of the Old Testament in the New,* 97) thinks of a broader application of "all flesh" because the gift of the Spirit extends to slaves (Joel 2:29), who would not normally be Israelites. However, slaves would still be counted as under the covenant (see Ex. 20:10; Deut. 12:12, 18; 16:11, 14).
43. Patterson, "Joel," 7:256.
44. Hubbard, *Joel and Amos: An Introduction and Commentary,* 71.
45. For example, Kaiser, *The Uses of the Old Testament in the New,* 97.
46. Ibid., 99–100.
47. Feinberg, *The Minor Prophets,* 82.
48. Kaiser, *The Uses of the Old Testament in the New,* 91.
49. Robert B. Chisholm, Jr., "Joel," in *The Bible Knowledge Commentary: Old Testament,* ed. John F. Walvoord and Roy B. Zuck (Wheaton, Ill.: Victor, 1985), 1421.
50. See Kaiser, *Toward an Old Testament Theology,* 268–69; Kenneth L. Barker, "False Dichotomies Between the Testaments," *Journal of the Evangelical Theological Society* 25 (1982): 10–15.
51. Barker ("False Dichotomies," 4, n. 5) refers to the type of interpretation advocated here as "progressive fulfillment," a label he says he borrowed from W. J. Beecher.
52. See also Paul D. Feinberg, "Hermeneutics of Discontinuity," in *Continuity and Discontinuity: Perspectives on the Relationship Between the Old and New Testaments,* ed. John S. Feinberg (Westchester, Ill.: Crossway, 1988), 108–28. He discusses clearly the hermeneutical issues and examines in more detail Peter's use of Joel 2:28–32, generally affirming Walter Kaiser's views.
53. Compare C. F. Keil, "Joel," in *Minor Prophets,* Commentary on the Old Testament in Ten Volumes (Reprint, Grand Rapids: Eerdmans, 1973), 220; Patterson, "Joel," 260.
54. James B. Pritchard, ed., *Ancient Near Eastern Texts Relating to the Old Testament,* 3d ed. (Princeton, N.J.: Princeton Univ. Press, 1969), 288.
55. Keil, "Joel," 220–21. Whereas the dispersion of the Jews under the Romans would be an additional instance of the atrocities spoken of by Joel, the events surrounding the fall of Jerusalem in 586 B.C. could account for his language in 3:1–6 more easily.
56. Feinberg, *The Minor Prophets,* 82. He says that Joel is "probably one of the earliest of the minor prophets" (p. 71).
57. Allen, *The Books of Joel, Obadiah, Jonah and Micah,* 110. For the political situation of Judah during the Exile, see, with some caution, Bustenay Oded, "Judah and the Exile," in *Israelite and Judean History,*

ed. John H. Hayes and J. Maxwell Miller (Philadelphia: Westminster, 1977), 476–80.

58. See Feinberg, *The Minor Prophets,* 83.
59. See Patterson, "Joel," 261.
60. See also K. Seybold, "gāmal; gāmûl; g^emûl; g^emûlāh; taghmûl" in *Theological Dictionary of the Old Testament, vol. 3,* ed. G. Johannes Botterweck and Helmer Ringgren (Grand Rapids: Eerdmans, 1975), 3:32.
61. Allen, *The Books of Joel, Obadiah, Jonah and Micah,* 114.
62. Chisholm, "Joel," 1422.
63. Bewer, "A Critical and Exegetical Commentary on Obadiah and Joel," 134.
64. Allen, *The Books of Joel, Obadiah, Jonah and Micah,* 115.
65. See Thomas J. Finley, "The Sheep Merchants of Zechariah 11," *Grace Theological Journal* 3 (1982): 51–65. But see also Kenneth L. Barker's remarks ("Zechariah," in *Expositor's Bible Commentary,* ed. Frank E. Gaebelein [Grand Rapids: Zondervan, 1985], 697).
66. Derek Kidner (*Genesis: An Introduction and Commentary,* Tyndale Old Testament Commentaries [Downers Grove, Ill.: InterVarsity, 1967], 219) applies the language of Jacob's blessing to "the golden age of the Coming One."
67. George A. Buttrick, ed. *Interpreter's Dictionary of the Bible* (Nashville: Abingdon, 1962), s.v. "Shittim."
68. *Fauna and Flora of the Bible,* Helps for Translators 11 (London: United Bible Societies, 1972), 87–88.
69. Allen, *The Books of Joel, Obadiah, Jonah and Micah,* 117.
70. See Feinberg, *The Minor Prophets,* 85.

Obadiah

1. See Ebenezer Henderson, *The Twelve Minor Prophets* (Grand Rapids: Baker, 1980), 186.
2. See Archer, *A Survey of Old Testament Introduction,* 335.
3. See David Clark and Norm Mundhenk, *A Translator's Handbook on the Books of Obadiah and Micah,* Helps for Translators (New York: United Bible Societies, 1982), 22.
4. Leon J. Wood, *The Prophets of Israel* (Grand Rapids: Baker, 1979), 263. See also Walter Baker ("Obadiah," in *The Bible Knowledge Commentary: Old Testament,* ed. John F. Walvoord and Roy B. Zuck [Wheaton: Victor, 1985], 1454), who thinks the reference to "fugitives" in Obadiah 14 would be incompatible with the events of 586 B.C. Whereas 2 Kings 25, 2 Chronicles 36, and Jeremiah 52 deal with Zedekiah's army (some of whom might have escaped; 2 Kings 25:5), they leave open the possibility of civilian refugees. The point of Obadiah 14 is that the Edomites do not allow the refugees to escape but hand them over to the enemy.

5. Archer, *A Survey of Old Testament Introduction,* 333–35; Wood, Prophets of Israel, 262–63. For an exhaustive list of all the historical possibilities, see Carl E. Armerding, "Obadiah," in *Expositor's Bible Commentary,* ed. Frank E. Gaebelein (Grand Rapids: Zondervan, 1985), 7:350–51.
6. See J. R. Bartlett, "The Rise and Fall of the Kingdom of Edom," *Palestine Exploration Quarterly* 104 (1972): 36–37.
7. Wood, *The Prophets of Israel,* 264.
8. C. F. Keil ("Obadiah," in *Minor Prophets,* Commentary on the Old Testament in Ten Volumes [Reprint, Grand Rapids: Eerdmans, 1973], 340–41) cites Caspari.
9. For more details, see Thomas J. Finley, *Joel, Amos, Obadiah,* Wycliffe Exegetical Commentary (Chicago: Moody, 1990), 342–45.
10. See Frank E. Gaebelein, *Four Minor Prophets: Obadiah, Jonah, Habakkuk, and Haggai* (Chicago: Moody, 1970), 15.
11. Perhaps the statement that Joab and the Israelites destroyed "all the men in Edom" (11:16) refers mainly to the army.
12. John Gray (*I & II Kings: A Commentary,* 2d ed., Old Testament Library [Philadelphia: Westminster, 1976], 605) suggests that Sela here does not refer to the capital of Edom but to some other place known by the same name, which means simply "rock, crag, cliff."
13. The Assyrian inscriptions also imply independence; see Pritchard, *Ancient Near Eastern Texts Relating to the Old Testament,* 282, 287, 291.
14. See Itzhaq Beit-Arieh ("New Light on the Edomites," *Biblical Archeology Review* 14 [1988]: 2:41) for interesting archeological evidence.
15. See Geoffrey W. Bromiley, ed., *International Standard Bible Encyclopedia,* rev. ed. (Grand Rapids: Eerdmans, 1979–1988), *s.v.* "Edom."
16. J. Alberto Soggin, *Introduction to the Old Testament,* 3d ed., Old Testament Library, trans. John Bowden (Louisville: Westminster/John Knox, 1989), 399.
17. See Kaiser, *Toward an Old Testament Theology,* 187; and Stuart, *Hosea–Jonah,* 404.
18. In Jeremiah 49:7 the placing of "To Edom" at the beginning of the verse forces the translation "Concerning Edom."
19. The NIV has "I will make you small," but "I have made you small" seems better at this point.
20. George A. Buttrick, ed., *The Interpreter's Dictionary of the Bible,* supplementary volume (Nashville: Abingdon, 1962), *s.v.* "Edom."
21. P. Kyle McCarter, "Obadiah 7 and the Fall of Edom," *Bulletin of the American Schools of Oriental Research* 220 (1975): 87–91. McCarter uses the historical evidence to date the book of Obadiah in the late sixth or early fifth century, but the statements are prophecy, not historical description.
22. Charles L. Feinberg, "Jeremiah," in *Expositor's Bible Commentary,* ed. Frank E. Gaebelein (Grand Rapids: Eerdmans, 1986), 560.
23. Allen, *The Books of Joel, Obadiah, Jonah and Micah,* 156–57.

24. See Ebenezer Henderson, *The Twelve Minor Prophets* (Grand Rapids: Baker, 1980), 195; Carl E. Armerding, "Obadiah," in *Expositor's Bible Commentary,* ed. Frank E. Gaebelein (Grand Rapids: Zondervan, 1985), 353; Leslie C. Allen, *The Books of Joel, Obadiah, Jonah and Micah,* New International Commentary on the Old Testament (Grand Rapids: Eerdmans, 1976), 161.
25. In Obadiah 13 the three occurrences of "their disaster," as translated by the NIV, are literally "their disaster" (once) and "his disaster," (twice) respectively.
26. Armerding, "Obadiah," 30.
27. J. R. Bartlett, "The Moabites and Edomites," in *Peoples of Old Testament Times,* ed. D. J. Wiseman (Oxford: Clarendon, 1975), 243–44.
28. See Jeffrey L. Townsend, "Fulfillment of the Land Promise in the Old Testament," *Bibliotheca Sacra* 142 (1985): 320–37. He has a helpful map on p. 327, but does not discuss this passage from Obadiah.
29. Geoffrey W. Bromiley, ed., *International Standard Bible Encyclopedia,* rev. ed. (Grand Rapids: Eerdmans, 1979–1988), *s.v.* "Negeb."
30. See Allen, *The Books of Joel, Obadiah, Jonah and Micah,* 171.
31. George A. Buttrick, ed., Interpreter's Dictionary of the Bible, supplementary volume (Nashville: Abingdon, 1962), *s.v.* "Sepharad."

MICAH

1. Some chronological issues are hard to resolve for these kings, especially with regard to the dates for Hezekiah's reign. See E. Thiele, *The Mysterious Numbers of the Hebrew Kings,* rev. ed. (Grand Rapids: Zondervan, 1983); G. L. Archer, "The Chronology of the Old Testament," in *Expositor's Bible Commentary,* ed. Frank E. Gaebelein (Grand Rapids: Zondervan, 1979), 1:369–71.
2. Compare Hosea 1:1, which mentions only Jeroboam II of Israel, omitting the names of six additional kings. Isaiah also did not mention any of the kings of Israel contemporary with him.
3. Most of the fixed dates given below are tentative; there are some significant chronological difficulties concerning the kings of Judah in the eighth century B.C. For details, see Archer, "Chronology of the Old Testament," 369–70; and J. N. Oswalt, "Chronology of the OT," in *The International Standard Bible Encyclopedia,* rev. ed., ed. Geoffrey W. Bromiley (Grand Rapids: Eerdmans, 1979), 1:681–84.
4. See Oswalt, "Chronology of the OT," 684.
5. Some think that the Hebrew "cause to pass through the fire" may mean something other than a literal child sacrifice. See M. Cogan and H. Tadmor, *II Kings,* Anchor Bible (New York: Doubleday, 1988), 11:266–67.
6. The chronological issues about Hezekiah's reign are well known. The main difficulty concerns 2 Kings 18:13, which seems to place the start of his reign at about 715 B.C., while other passages require a date of about 728 B.C. If he ruled simultaneously with his father, that would solve

most of the problems. Other solutions include assuming that the original text of 2 Kings 18:13 read twenty-four years instead of fourteen or that the chronological notice has been misplaced from 2 Kings 20:1. See Archer, "The Chronology of the Old Testament," 370; Oswalt, "Chronology of the OT," 684; and Cogan and Tadmor, *II Kings,* 228.

7. See Pritchard, *Ancient Near Eastern Texts Relating to the Old Testament,* 288.
8. An Asherah was probably a pole erected to symbolize the fertility goddess Asherah, known in the texts discovered at Ras Shamra (Ugarit) as the consort of El, the supreme god (Geoffrey W. Bromiley, ed., *International Standard Bible Encyclopedia,* rev. ed. [Grand Rapids: Eerdmans, 1979–1988], s.v. "Asherah").
9. Bernhard Anderson (*The Eighth Century Prophets,* Proclamation Commentaries [Philadelphia: Fortress, 1978], 43) is right to stress the importance of social relationships in defining justice for the prophets of the eighth century B.C., but it seems a false dichotomy to set that emphasis over against "behavior that conforms to an ethical or legal norm."
10. Feinberg, *The Minor Prophets,* 53; see also Allen, *The Books of Joel, Obadiah, Jonah and Micah,* 257–61; and Bruce K. Waltke, "Micah," in *The Minor Prophets,* ed. Thomas Edward McComiskey (Grand Rapids: Baker, 1993), 2:594.
11. James Luther Mays, *Micah: A Commentary,* Old Testament Library (Philadelphia: Westminster, 1976), 3.
12. C. F. Keil, "Micah," in *Minor Prophets,* Commentary on the Old Testament in Ten Volumes (reprint, Grand Rapids: Eerdmans, 1973), 425.
13. Allen, *The Books of Joel, Obadiah, Jonah and Micah,* 269.
14. Several factors complicate the listing of the twelve tribes of Israel. Some lists include Joseph's two sons, Ephraim and Manasseh, and exclude Levi, which was considered the Lord's special possession (see Num. 1). Also, Simeon had evidently assimilated into Judah by the time of David (see Josh. 19:1; 1 Chron. 4:28–33; Geoffrey W. Bromiley, ed., *The International Standard Bible Encyclopedia,* rev. ed. [Grand Rapids: Eerdmans, 1979–1988], s.v. "Simeon").
15. The Bible ascribes the fall of Samaria to Shalmaneser V (2 Kings 17:3–6), but Sargon II, his successor, claims the feat for himself in his annals. According to R. M. Talbert ("Assyria and Babylonia," in *The Interpreter's Dictionary of the Bible,* supplementary volume, ed. George A. Buttrick [Nashville: Abingdon, 1976], 5:75), "Re-evaluation of the evidence indicates that [Sargon's] scribes altered the historical record." It is also possible that Sargon engaged in "mopping-up" operations.
16. Only later does "Samaria" mean a province, as in the New Testament.
17. N. Avigad, "Samaria," in *Encyclopedia of Archaeological Excavations in the Holy Land,* ed. Michael Avi-Yonah (Englewood Cliffs, N.J.: Prentice-Hall, 1978), 4:1046.
18. Allen, *The Books of Joel, Obadiah, Jonah and Micah,* 274.
19. Ibid., 274–75.
20. See also Pritchard, *Ancient Near Eastern Texts,* 282–84.

21. Charles S. Shaw, "Micah 1:10–16 Reconsidered," *Journal of Biblical Literature* 106 (1987): 223–29.
22. Allen, *The Books of Joel, Obadiah, Jonah and Micah,* 280.
23. Ibid., 281.
24. Ibid. Another thought is that the "Daughter of Zion" is the "you" of v. 15. It seems abrupt to read it that way, but compare Waltke ("Micah," 2:155): "Judah's rulers must give as a dowry (= the hated tribute) the town once betrothed to them, but now pledged to the enemy."
25. For another view see Allen, *The Books of Joel, Obadiah, Jonah and Micah,* 282.
26. See Keil, "Micah," 437.
27. Ibid.
28. "He who" in the NIV is inferred from the Hebrew; the interpretation given here is also possible.
29. Pritchard, *Ancient Near Eastern Texts,* 288.
30. Keil, "Micah," 437; Allen, *The Books of Joel, Obadiah, Jonah and Micah,* 283.
31. See Christopher J. H. Wright, *An Eye for an Eye: The Place of Old Testament Ethics Today* (Downers Grove, Ill.: InterVarsity, 1983), 38–39, 57–59.
32. Allen, *The Books of Joel, Obadiah, Jonah and Micah,* 291.
33. It is not always clear in the prophets when the Lord speaks directly and when the prophet does so. "My" probably refers to the Lord here; "my blessing" in 2:9 would be strange if it were the prophet's blessing. Through inspiration, of course, the words even of the prophet are ultimately from the Lord.
34. Literally, "from the front of a garment they strip off splendor." Since the Hebrew word for "splendor" is very close to another word meaning "coat," the phrase might refer to stealing a coat. Possibly it means that they took something costly or beautiful from the front of the garment.
35. David Clark and Norm Mundhenk, *A Translator's Handbook on the Books of Obadiah and Micah,* Helps for Translators (New York: United Bible Societies, 1982), 91.
36. Allen (*The Books of Joel, Obadiah, Jonah and Micah,* 302–3) sees a reference to Sennacherib's blockade against Jerusalem, which God Himself broke. Whereas some similarities exist for a point of comparison, the language of gathering all of Jacob and the remnant of Israel together makes a future kingdom setting more likely.
37. Feinberg, *The Minor Prophets,* 162.
38. The Hebrew has an uncommon term for "ruler" here. It often means a military commander (Josh. 10:24; Judg. 11:6), but Micah and Isaiah use it for political leadership (see Isa. 1:10; 3:6).
39. Divination: "the art or science of deducing the future or the unknown through the observation and interpretation of some facet of nature or human life, ordinarily of an unpredictable and trivial character" (Geoffrey W. Bromiley, ed., *International Standard Bible Encyclopedia,* rev. ed. [Grand Rapids: Eerdmans, 1979–1988], s.v. "Divination").

40. John N. Oswalt, "nn (Khh)" *Theological Wordbook of the Old Testament,* ed. R. Laird Harris et al. (Chicago: Moody, 1980), 436–37.
41. H. Kosmala, "gābhar; gᵉbhûrāh; gᵉbhir; gibbôr; gebher" in *Theological Dictionary of the Old Testament, vol. 2,* ed. G. Johannes Botterweck and Helmer Ringgren (Grand Rapids: Eerdmans, 1975), 2:370.
42. Some have thought it too abrupt to have been written by Micah. Because of the similarities with Isaiah 2:2–5, James Luther Mays (*Micah: A Commentary,* Old Testament Library [Philadelphia: Westminster, 1976], 95–96) could be correct in contending that both prophets incorporated this saying from an earlier source. The section does have some close connections with Micah 3 (see Waltke, "Micah," 2:676), however, and it may well be that the prophecy originated with Micah (see also Feinberg, *The Minor Prophets,* 167).
43. Deuteronomy 31:29 applies the same expression in the original language ("in days to come" {NIV]) to the time of judgment for disobedience.
44. The Dome of the Rock and the Mosque of Al Aqsa are currently located here.
45. Waltke ("Micah," 678–79) thinks of the temple mount towering over all the mountains of the world, including Everest. This is possible, but not strictly demanded by the language of the text.
46. "The remnant of men" found in Acts 15:17 is based on an alternate reading of the Hebrew letters for "Edom" that is found in the ancient Greek translation of the Old Testament (Septuagint).
47. Waltke, "Micah," 680.
48. Ibid., 683.
49. See Deuteronomy 22:1 and Ezekiel 34:4, where the word "straying" or "strays" is the same term under discussion here. It is also rendered "banished" (Deut. 30:4; 2 Sam. 14:13–14), "exiled" or "exiles" (Neh. 1:9; Ps. 147:2; Isa. 11:12; 27:13; 56:8; Jer. 49:36), "fugitives" (Isa. 16:3–4), "outcast" (Jer. 30:17), and "driven away" (Jer. 49:5).
50. I have followed the ancient division of the Hebrew text, which shows a major break between 4:7 and 4:8. Others prefer to start the new paragraph with 4:9.
51. David Noel Freedman, ed., *The Anchor Bible Dictionary* (New York: Doubleday, 1992), s.v. "Eder, Tower of."
52. Feinberg, *Minor Prophets,* 170.
53. Freedman, ed., *The Anchor Bible Dictionary,* s.v. "Ophel."
54. Elaine R. Follis, "The Holy City as Daughter," in *Directions in Biblical Hebrew Poetry,* ed. Elaine R. Follis, *Journal for the Study of the Old Testament Supplements* 40 (Sheffield: Sheffield Academic Press, 1987), 178.
55. The word *now* helps to mark the separate prophecies (4:9, 11). An additional "now" occurs in 5:1, but the Hebrew term is left untranslated in the NIV.
56. Feinberg, *The Minor Prophets,* 171.
57. Some think that the ruler (lit. "judge") of 5:1 already refers to the Messiah. Feinberg (*The Minor Prophets,* 172) gives several reasons why it

does not refer to Jesus Christ. There could be a typological reference to the fact that Jesus was struck on the face (Luke 22:64; John 18:22), but the historical person behind the type would have to be a king who was struck according to the circumstances that Micah describes.

58. Waltke, "Micah," 702.
59. In the city list of Joshua 15, the Greek Old Testament (Septuagint) includes it after verse 59. See the RSV.
60. Waltke, "Micah," 705.
61. In all of these instances the NASB has "days of old."
62. Waltke, "Micah," 705.
63. Feinberg, *The Minor Prophets,* 173; Thomas Edward McComiskey, "Micah," in *Expositor's Bible Commentary,* ed. Frank E. Gaebelein (Grand Rapids: Zondervan, 1985), 7:427.
64. McComiskey, "Micah," 480–81. See also D. K. Innes ("Some Notes on Micah," *Evangelical Quarterly* 41, no. 3 [1969]: 170): "These words are suited to convey both the ancient lineage of Christ as a descendant of the family of David, and also His eternal preexistence."
65. In Hebrew the term for "Assyria" is the same as that for "Asshur," the person. Thus, the KJV of Genesis 10:11 is possible: "Out of that land went forth Asshur . . . ." Then it is hard to explain, though, why 10:10 refers to "the first centers of his kingdom," if Nimrod did not also build centers in Assyria.
66. Feinberg, *The Minor Prophets,* 175.
67. See Finley, *Joel, Amos, Obadiah,* 137–38.
68. Feinberg, *The Minor Prophets,* 175–76; and Waltke, "Micah," 712–13.
69. McComiskey, "Micah," 430–31.
70. The standard interpretation is that 6:1–5 has the form of the "prophetic lawsuit," whereas 6:6–8 takes its form from a situation wherein the worshiper would arrive at the temple and ask the priest what he or she must do to get into the sanctuary (see Pss. 15; 24:3–5; Allen, *The Books of Joel, Obadiah, Jonah and Micah,* 369; and Waltke, "Micah," 2:726).
71. This difference is brought out by the archaic forms of "you" found in the KJV. A simple rule of thumb makes it easy to observe the distinction when using that version. All the forms that begin with "th" (thou, thee, thy) refer to only one person, whereas all the forms that begin with "y" (ye, you, your) refer to more than one person.
72. Clark and Mundhenk, *A Translator's Handbook on the Books of Obadiah and Micah,* 153–54.
73. Waltke, "Micah," 2:728.
74. Feinberg, *The Minor Prophets,* 177.
75. The ancient Jewish paraphrase in the Aramaic language (Targum) says, "I sent my three prophets to you: Moses to teach traditions and laws; Aaron to make atonement for the people; and Miriam to instruct the women."
76. A fascinating inscription outside the Bible that refers to Balaam has been discovered in the East Jordan Valley: see David Noel Freedman, ed., *The Anchor Bible Dictionary* (New York: Doubleday, 1992), s.v.

"Deir 'Alla, Tell: Texts," 2:129–30; Archer, *A Survey of Old Testament Introduction,* 270.

77. Waltke, "Micah," 2:733.
78. Allen, *The Books of Joel, Obadiah, Jonah and Micah,* 371.
79. The place name *Adam* occurs in Joshua 3:16; the NRSV reads the place name also at Hosea 6:7.
80. Other verses where the NASB has "loyalty" but the NIV has "love" include Proverbs 20:6, 28; 21:21; Hosea 6:4, 6.
81. S. Dawes, "Walking Humbly: Micah 6.8 Revisited," *Scottish Journal of Theology* 41, no. 3 (1988): 332–33.
82. The preface to the NIV indicates that in such cases it was not usually considered necessary to notify the reader if an alternate reading was adopted.
83. Kathleen Kenyon, *Royal Cities of the Old Testament* (New York: Schocken, 1971), 76.
84. Feinberg, *The Minor Prophets,* 181.
85. Feinberg, *The Minor Prophets,* 182; Waltke, "Micah," 2:748. The TEV additionally takes "your" to refer to the people.
86. Waltke ("Micah," 2:748) says Micah gives here "specific illustrations of the confusion, the social anarchy, in the besieged city."
87. Waltke, "Micah," 2:748–49.
88. The Hebrew feminine form for "your" in verse 10 shows that the speaker in these verses is a woman. Also Micah's response to her speech in verses 11–13 uses feminine forms for "you" and "your."
89. Feinberg, *The Minor Prophets,* 183. The ancient Jewish translation into the Aramaic language (Targum) has, "Do not rejoice over me, O Romans my enemy."
90. Ibid., 184–85.
91. Mays, *Micah: A Commentary,* 164. The TEV, JB, and NRSV all imply this view.
92. Feinberg, *The Minor Prophets*, 185.
93. The NRSV changes the text so that Micah's prayer seems to continue: "show us marvelous things." Whereas only a minor change in the Hebrew is needed to get that reading, it does not seem necessary in light of Micah's style.
94. Clark and Mundhenk (*A Translator's Handbook on the Books of Obadiah and Micah,* 193) see a structural pattern in vv. 18–19 that focuses on His "delight to show mercy."

BIBLIOGRAPHY

Allen, Leslie C. *The Books of Joel, Obadiah, Jonah and Micah.* New International Commentary on the Old Testament. Grand Rapids: Eerdmans, 1976.

Anderson, Bernhard. *The Eighth Century Prophets: Amos, Hosea, Isaiah, Micah.* Proclamation Commentaries. Philadelphia: Fortress, 1978.

Archer, Gleason L., Jr. "The Chronology of the Old Testament." In *Expositor's Bible Commentary*, edited by Frank E. Gaebelein, 1:359–74. Grand Rapids: Zondervan, 1979.

_______. *A Survey of Old Testament Introduction*, revised and expanded. Chicago: Moody, 1994.

Armerding, Carl E. "Obadiah." In *Expositor's Bible Commentary*, edited by Frank E. Gaebelein, 7:333–57. Grand Rapids: Zondervan, 1985.

Baker, Walter. "Obadiah." In *The Bible Knowledge Commentary: Old Testament*, edited by John F. Walvoord and Roy B. Zuck, 1453–59. Wheaton, Ill.: Victor, 1985.

Barker, Kenneth L. "False Dichotomies Between the Testaments." *Journal of the Evangelical Theological Society* 25 (1982): 1:10–15.

_______. *The NIV. The Making of a Contemporary Translation.* Grand Rapids: Zondervan, 1986.

_______. "Zechariah." In *Expositor's Bible Commentary*, edited by Frank E. Gaebelein, 7:593–697. Grand Rapids: Zondervan, 1985.

Bewer, Julius A. "A Critical and Exegetical Commentary on Obadiah and Joel." In *A Critical and Exegetical Commentary on Micah, Zephaniah, Nahum, Habakkuk, Obadiah and Joel.* 1911. Reprint. Edinburgh: T & T Clark, 1974.

Botterweck, G. Johannes, and Helmer Ringgren, eds. *Theological Dictionary of the Old Testament.* Grand Rapids: Eerdmans, 1975.

Bromiley, Geoffrey W., ed. *The International Standard Bible Encyclopedia.* Rev. ed. Grand Rapids: Eerdmans, 1979–1988.

Buttrick, George A., ed. *Interpreter's Dictionary of the Bible.* Nashville: Abingdon, 1962.

Calvin, John. *Joel, Amos, Obadiah.* Vol. 2 of *Commentaries on the Twelve Minor Prophets.* Translated by John Owen. Grand Rapids: Baker, 1981.

Chisholm, Robert B., Jr. "Joel." In *The Bible Knowledge Commentary: Old Testament*, edited by John F. Walvoord and Roy B. Zuck, 1409–24. Wheaton, Ill.: Victor, 1985.

_______. "Wordplay in the Eighth-Century Prophets." *Bibliotheca Sacra* 144 (1987): vol. 144, no. 573, 44–52.

Clark, David, and Norm Mundhenk. *A Translator's Handbook on the Books of Obadiah and Micah.* Helps for Translators. New York: United Bible Societies, 1982.

Cogan, Mordechai, and Hayim Tadmor. *II Kings: A New Translation with Introduction and Commentary.* Vol. 11 of Anchor Bible. New York: Doubleday, 1988.

Dawes, S. "Walking Humbly: Micah 6:8 Revisited." *Scottish Journal of Theology* 41, no. 3 (1988): 331–39.

Driver, S. R. *The Books of Joel and Amos.* Cambridge Bible for Schools and Colleges. Cambridge: Cambridge Univ. Press, 1907.

Eissfeldt, Otto. *The Old Testament: An Introduction.* Translated by Peter R. Ackroyd. New York: Harper & Row, 1972.

Fauna and Flora of the Bible. Vol. 11 of Helps for Translators. London: United Bible Societies, 1972.

Feinberg, Charles L. "Jeremiah." In *Expositor's Bible Commentary*, edited by Frank E. Gaebelein, 6:355–691. Grand Rapids: Eerdmans, 1986.

________. *The Minor Prophets.* Chicago: Moody, 1976.

Feinberg, Paul D. "Hermeneutics of Discontinuity." In *Continuity and Discontinuity: Perspectives on the Relationship Between the Old and New Testaments,* edited by John S. Feinberg. Westchester, Ill.: Crossway, 1988.

Finley, Thomas J. *Joel, Amos, Obadiah.* Wycliffe Exegetical Commentary. Chicago: Moody, 1990.

________. "The Sheep Merchants of Zechariah 11." *Grace Theological Journal* 3 (1982): 51–65.

Follis, Elaine R. "The Holy City as Daughter." In *Directions in Biblical Hebrew Poetry*, edited by Elaine R. Follis. *Journal for the Study of the Old Testament Supplements* 40. Sheffield: Sheffield Academic Press, 1987.

Freedman, David Noel, ed. *The Anchor Bible Dictionary.* New York: Doubleday, 1992.

Gaebelein, Frank E. *Four Minor Prophets: Obadiah, Jonah, Habakkuk, and Haggai; Their Message for Today.* Chicago: Moody, 1970.

Gray, John. *I & II Kings: A Commentary.* 2d ed. Old Testament Library. Philadelphia: Westminster, 1976.

Harris, R. Laird et al., eds. *Theological Wordbook of the Old Testament.* Chicago: Moody, 1980.

Harrison, Roland Kenneth. *Introduction to the Old Testament.* Grand Rapids: Eerdmans, 1969.

Henderson, Ebenezer. *The Twelve Minor Prophets: Translated from the Original Hebrew with a Critical and Exegetical Commentary.* Grand Rapids: Baker, 1980.

Hubbard, David Allan. *Joel and Amos: An Introduction and Commentary.* Tyndale Old Testament Commentaries. Downers Grove, Ill.: InterVarsity, 1989.

Innes, D. K. "Some Notes on Micah." *Evangelical Quarterly* 41, no. 1 (1969): 10–13; no. 2: 108–111; no. 3: 169–71; no. 4: 216–20.

Kaiser, Walter C., Jr. *Toward an Old Testament Theology*. Grand Rapids: Zondervan, 1978.

_______. *The Uses of the Old Testament in the New*. Chicago: Moody, 1985.

Keil, C. F. "Joel." In *Minor Prophets*. Commentary on the Old Testament in Ten Volumes. Reprint. Grand Rapids: Eerdmans, 1973.

_______. "Micah." In *Minor Prophets*. Commentary on the Old Testament in Ten Volumes. Reprint. Grand Rapids: Eerdmans, 1973.

_______. "Obadiah." In *Minor Prophets*. Commentary on the Old Testament in Ten Volumes. Reprint. Grand Rapids: Eerdmans, 1973.

Kenyon, Kathleen. *Royal Cities of the Old Testament*. New York: Schocken, 1971.

Kidner, Derek. *Genesis: An Introduction and Commentary*. Tyndale Old Testament Commentaries. Downers Grove, Ill.: InterVarsity, 1967.

Mallon, Elias D. "A Stylistic Analysis of Joel 1:10–12." *Catholic Biblical Quarterly* 45 (1983): 537–48.

Mays, James Luther. *Micah: A Commentary*. Old Testament Library. Philadelphia: Westminster, 1976.

McCarter, P. Kyle. "Obadiah 7 and the Fall of Edom." *Bulletin of the American Schools of Oriental Research* 220 (1975): 87–91.

McComiskey, Thomas Edward. "Micah." In *Expositor's Bible Commentary*, edited by Frank E. Gaebelein, 7:393–445. Grand Rapids: Zondervan, 1985.

Oswalt, J. N. "Chronology of the OT." In *The International Standard Bible Encyclopedia*. Rev. ed., edited by Geoffrey W. Bromiley, 1:673–85. Grand Rapids: Eerdmans, 1979.

Patterson, Richard D. "Joel." In *Expositor's Bible Commentary*, edited by Frank E. Gaebelein, 7:227–66. Grand Rapids: Zondervan, 1985.

Price, Walter K. *The Prophet Joel and the Day of the Lord*. Chicago: Moody, 1976.

Pritchard, James B., ed. *Ancient Near Eastern Texts Relating to the Old Testament*. 3d ed. Princeton, N.J.: Princeton Univ. Press, 1969.

Shaw, Charles S. "Micah 1:10–16 Reconsidered." *Journal of Biblical Literature* 106 (1987): 2:223–29.

Soggin, J. Alberto. *Introduction to the Old Testament: From Its Origins to the Closing of the Alexandrine Canon*. 3d ed., translated by John Bowden. Old Testament Library. Louisville: Westminster/John Knox, 1989.

Stuart, Douglas. *Hosea–Jonah*. Word Biblical Commentary 31. Waco, Tex.: Word, 1987.

Talbert, R. M. "Assyria and Babylonia." In *The Interpreter's Dictionary of the Bible,* supplementary volume. Edited by George A. Buttrick, 5: 73–76 xxx–xx. Nashville: Abingdon, 1976.

Thiele, Edwin R. *The Mysterious Numbers of the Hebrew Kings*. Rev. ed. Grand Rapids: Zondervan, 1983.

Waltke, Bruce K. "Micah." In *The Minor Prophets: An Exegetical and Expository Commentary,* edited by Thomas Edward McComiskey, 2:591–764. Grand Rapids: Baker, 1993.

Wenham, Gordon J. *The Book of Leviticus*. New International Commentary on the Old Testament. Grand Rapids: Eerdmans, 1979.

Wolff, Hans Walter. *Joel and Amos*. Translated by Waldemar Janzen et al. Hermeneia. Philadelphia: Fortress, 1977.

Wood, Leon J. *The Prophets of Israel*. Grand Rapids: Baker, 1979.

Wright, Christopher J. H. *An Eye for an Eye: The Place of Old Testament Ethics Today*. Downers Grove, Ill.: InterVarsity, 1983.

Young, E. J. *Introduction to the Old Testament*. Grand Rapids: Eerdmans, 1949.

Moody Press, a ministry of Moody Bible Institute,
is designed for education, evangelization, and edification.
If we may assist you in knowing more about Christ
and the Christian life, please write us without obligation:
Moody Press, c/o MLM, Chicago, Illinois 60610.